Android Game Recipes

J. F. DiMarzio

Apress

Android Game Recipes

ISBN-13 (pbk): 978-1-4302-5764-6

ISBN-13 (electronic): 978-1-4302-5765-3

President and Publisher: Paul Manning
Lead Editor: Michelle Lowman
Technical Reviewer: Jim Graham
Editorial Board: Steve Anglin, Mark Beckner, Ewan Buckingham, Gary Cornell, Louise Corrigan, Morgan Ertel, Jonathan Gennick, Jonathan Hassell, Robert Hutchinson, Michelle Lowman, James Markham, Matthew Moodie, Jeff Olson, Jeffrey Pepper, Douglas Pundick, Ben Renow-Clarke, Dominic Shakeshaft, Gwenan Spearing, Matt Wade, Tom Welsh, Steve Weiss, James T. DeWolf
Coordinating Editor: Christine Ricketts
Copy Editor: Vanessa Moore
Compositor: SPi Global
Indexer: SPi Global
Artist: SPi Global
Cover Designer: Anna Ishchenko

Distributed to the book trade worldwide by Springer Science+Business Media New York, 233 Spring Street, 6th Floor, New York, NY 10013. Phone 1-800-SPRINGER, fax (201) 348-4505, e-mail orders-ny@springer-sbm.com, or visit www.springeronline.com. Apress Media, LLC is a California LLC and the sole member (owner) is Springer Science + Business Media Finance Inc (SSBM Finance Inc). SSBM Finance Inc is a Delaware corporation.

For information on translations, please e-mail rights@apress.com, or visit www.apress.com.

Apress and friends of ED books may be purchased in bulk for academic, corporate, or promotional use. eBook versions and licenses are also available for most titles. For more information, reference our Special Bulk Sales–eBook Licensing web page at www.apress.com/bulk-sales.

Any source code or other supplementary materials referenced by the author in this text is available to readers at www.apress.com. For detailed information about how to locate your book's source code, go to www.apress.com/source-code/.

This book is dedicated to the memory of Ben Eagle. Ben was a great colleague and the illustrator for many of the figures in my Android gaming books.

Contents at a Glance

Contents

About the Author

J. F. DiMarzio is a seasoned Android developer and author. He began developing games in Basic on the TRS-80 Color Computer II in 1984. Since then, DiMarzio has worked in the technology departments of institutions such as the U.S. Department of Defense and the Walt Disney Company. He has been developing on the Android platform since the beta release of version .03, and he has published two professional applications and one game on the Android Market.

About the Technical Reviewer

Jim Graham received a Bachelor of Science in electronics with a specialty in telecommunications from Texas A&M and graduated with his class (Class of '88) in 1989. He was published in the International Communications Association's 1988 issue of ICA Communique ("Fast Packet Switching: An Overview of Theory and Performance"). His work experience includes working as an associate network engineer in the Network Design Group at Amoco Corporation in Chicago, IL; a senior network engineer at Tybrin Corporation in Fort Walton Beach, FL; and as an intelligence systems analyst at both 16th Special Operations Wing Intelligence and HQ US Air Force Special Operations Command Intelligence at Hurlburt Field, FL. He received a formal letter of commendation from the 16th Special Operations Wing Intelligence on December 18, 2001.

Acknowledgments

The author would like to acknowledge everyone who helped to create this book, including my agent Neil Salkind and everyone at Studio B, all of the editors at Apress for their wonderfull support during the publishing process, and my illustrator Ben Eagle.

Introduction

Welcome to *Android Game Recipes*. This book is specifically written to help you with many of the common problems that you may have encountered while in the process of creating a game for the Android platform. Android game development can be a fun, enjoyable, and rewarding process; but it is not without its pitfalls. There always seem to be problems that come up during the development process that are difficult to find solutions to. My hope is that this book can provide you with those solutions.

I have created multiple games for Android, and have encountered many problems while doing so. My experiences, and the solutions I have found, are compiled into 17 chapters, each separated by major topic. Outlined as follows are the chapters in this book and a quick summary of what will be covered in each.

Chapter 1: Getting Started. This chapter covers the skills and software that you need to make the most of this book. Chapter 1 also includes a quick introduction to Android gaming and OpenGL ES versions 1, and 2 / 3.

Chapter 2: Loading an Image. There are different situations that may call for an image to be loaded either with or without OpenGL ES. If you are creating a splash screen you may not want to use OpenGL. The recipes in this chapter help you create a splash screen without using OpenGL.

Chapter 3: The Splash Screen. Here you'll find solutions to common problems in creating splash screens. These problems can include loading the screen image, transitions between multiple images, and loading the game after the splash screen.

Chapter 4: The Menu Screen. In this chapter, you'll learn solutions to common menu screen problems, such as creating buttons, loading options, locking screen rotation, and detecting screen resolution.

Chapter 5: Reading Player Input. The recipes in this chapter solve problems related to reading player input during the game, such as touch screen input, multi touch, and gestures.

Chapter 6: Loading a SpriteSheet. Being able to load a spritesheet is essential in creating a game. This chapter contains solutions for loading spritesheet images, animating multiple spritesheet images, and storing spritesheets.

Chapter 7: Scrolling a Background. Key to realism, Chapter 7 helps you solve issues related to scrolling a background image on the screen, such as loading the image to the screen and changing the scroll speed.

Chapter 8: Scrolling Multiple Backgrounds. In this chapter you'll encounter recipes for how to scroll multiple background images to give the appearance of a foreground, middleground, and distance.

Chapter 9: Syncing a Background to Character Movement. In this chapter you'll find solutions for changing the direction and speed of the background movement in relationship to the movement of the character.

Chapter 10: Building a Level Using Tiles. You'll learn how to create levels for side-scrolling and platform games from graphic tiles. Using repeatable tiles is a tried and tested way to create game levels.

Chapter 11: Moving a Character. This covers problems that could arise when trying to animate a playable character, everything from walking, to running, to jumping and fighting.

Chapter 12: Moving an Enemy. Like Chapter 11, this chapter also discusses moving characters across the screen. However, this chapter focuses more on the specific problems encountered when creating AI based (non-playable) characters, such as moving on a predetermined path.

Chapter 13: Moving a Character with Obstacles. Most games do not have a smooth surface for which to play. That is, many game levels contain obstacles and inclines that the player needs to navigate. In this chapter you'll encounter recipes for how to let your playable character navigate these obstacles.

Chapter 14: Firing Weapons. In this chapter you'll learn how to fire or throw weapons. There are specific problems that need to be addressed when animating projectiles that include animation and the calculation of trajectories.

Chapter 15: Collision Detection. A key topic in game development, this covers the complex issue of collision detection. You'll find recipes for how to detect and react to interactions between onscreen (in-game) objects.

Chapter 16: Keeping Score. One way for a player to track their process in a game is through a score. The solutions in chapter 16 help you compile a gamer's score and write that score to the screen.

Chapter 17: Keeping Time. Some games are time based, or contain time based levels and challenges. Chapter 17 covers solutions for how to implement and track the expiration of time for marshaling in-game action.

Getting Started

Welcome to *Android Game Recipes*. This book is very much like a cookbook. It is designed to tackle specific, common problems that could arise while you develop a game for the Android platform. Solutions are provided in a well-tested, thought-out approach that is easy to follow and easy to adapt to multiple situations.

Let's say you know the theory behind what goes into chicken soup, but you are unsure how to turn some chicken and vegetables into soup. Consulting a standard, kitchen cookbook would give you a step-by-step recipe to create the soup. In much the same way, you will be able to use *Android Game Recipes* to find out exactly how to code specific scenarios in a game—from creating a splash screen to using collision detection when destroying an enemy.

Before you move on to the recipes, it's important to establish the proper framework to get the most out of them. In this chapter, we will discuss what skills and tools you will need to get the most out of this book.

What You Will Need

Game programming, as a discipline, is complex and can take years to master. However, the basic concepts of game programming are actually relatively simple to learn and can be reused in many situations. The amount of time that you put into your games and your code will ultimately determine how successful you and your games are. Everyone runs into that one problem when coding which, no matter how long you scratch your head, or how many times you search on Google, you just cannot get an exact solution for. This book is designed to be your solution to many of these problems.

Skills and Experience

This book is not aimed at beginners or people who have no game development experience. You will not learn how to develop an entire game from scratch by reading this book. This is not to say that you need to be a professional game developer to use this book. To the contrary, it is assumed that by reading this book you are most likely a casual game developer; you are likely to be someone who might have tried to create a game or two (possibly even for Android) and has run into a problem converting some of your development knowledge to the Android platform.

This book is focused on helping you through specific problems or scenarios. Therefore, you should have at least a working knowledge of game development, and at least a basic knowledge of Android-specific development. Neither topic will be covered from the perspective of a "from scratch" primer.

Since Android is developed in Java, you should also possess a good, working knowledge of Java development. There will be no tutorials on how Java works, and it may be implied during certain scenarios that you know the meaning behind the structure of Java.

It is possible however, that you may have some game development experience on another platform—such as Windows—and possibly even some business-level Java experience, and never have used OpenGL ES. Most of the time, developing a game for Android will require use of OpenGL ES. For this reason, the second part of this chapter is dedicated to introducing you to OpenGL ES and explaining why it is important to Android. If you already have experience with OpenGL ES, feel free to skip that part of this chapter, "OpenGL ES at a Glance."

In short, if you have a passion for game development and a passion for Android, but are running into some problems in your development, this book is for you. Whether you have already started to develop a game and are running into problems, or you are in the beginning stages of your development and are unsure what to do next, *Android Games Development Recipes* will guide you through the most common roadblocks and issues.

Software Versions

At this point, you are probably ready to dive right into finding solutions for your Android game scenarios. So what tools do you need to begin your journey?

This book is geared toward Android 4.1 and 4.2 Jelly Bean. If you are not working in Jelly Bean, it is recommended that you upgrade your SDK at http://developer.android.com/sdk/. However, the examples should also work on Android 4.0 Ice Cream Sandwich. There are many resources to help you download and install the SDK (and the corresponding Java components that you might need) if you need help doing so; however, this book will not cover installing the SDK.

You will also be using the Kepler version of Eclipse. One of the great features of Eclipse is that it will support multiple versions of Android SDKs. Therefore, you can quickly test your code in Jelly Bean, Ice Cream Sandwich, or even Gingerbread if needed. While you can use almost any Java IDE or text editor to write Android code, I prefer Eclipse because of features such as this and the well-crafted plug-ins that tightly integrate to many of the more tedious manual operations of compiling and debugging Android code. After all, Eclipse is the official Android development IDE recommended by Google, the creator of Android.

If you do not already have Eclipse Kepler, and want to give it a try, it is a free download from http://eclipse.org.

This book will not dive into the download or setup of Eclipse. There are many resources, including those on Eclipse's own site and the Android Developer's Forum, that can help you set up your environment should you require assistance.

> **Tip** If you have never installed Eclipse or a similar IDE, follow the installation directions carefully. The last thing you want is an incorrectly installed IDE impeding your ability to write great games.

In the next section, we will explore one of the most used tools in creating games on the Android platform, OpenGL ES.

OpenGL ES at a Glance

OpenGL ES, or OpenGL for Embedded Systems, is an open source graphics API that is packaged with the Android SDK. While there is limited support for working with graphics using core Android calls, it would be extremely difficult—if not impossible—to create an entire game without using OpenGL ES. Core Android graphics calls are slow and clunky, and with few exceptions, should not be used for gaming. This is where OpenGL ES comes in.

OpenGL ES has been included with Android, in one form or another, since the very beginning of the platform. In earlier versions of Android, the implementation of OpenGL ES was a limited version of OpenGL ES 1. As Android grew, and versions of Android matured, more feature-rich implementations of OpenGL ES were added. With Android version Jelly Bean, developers have access to OpenGL ES 2 for game development.

So what exactly does OpenGL ES do for you, and how does it do it? Let's find out.

How OpenGL ES Works with Android

Open GL ES communicates with the graphic hardware in a much more direct manner than a core Android call. This means that you are sending data directly to the hardware that is responsible for processing it. A core Android call would have to go through the core Android processes, threads, and interpreter before getting to the graphics hardware. Games written for the Android platform can only achieve an acceptable level of speed and playability by communicating directly with the GPU (Graphics Processing Unit).

Current versions of Android have the ability to use either OpenGL ES 1 or OpenGL ES 2 / 3 calls. There is a big difference between the two versions, and which one you use will play a role in determining who can run your game, and who will not be able to.

> **Note** All of the examples in this book that include OpenGL ES code are given in both OpenGL ES version 1 and OpenGL ES version 2 / 3.

OpenGL ES facilitates this interaction between your game and the graphics hardware in one of two different ways. The type of GPU employed in the Android device running your game will determine which version of OpenGL ES you use, thus how OpenGL will interact with the hardware. There are two major kinds of graphics hardware in the market, and because they are very different, two different versions of OpenGL ES are required to interact with them.

The two different types of hardware are those with a fixed-function pipeline, and those with shaders. The next few sections quickly review OpenGL ES and fixed-function pipelines, and OpenGL ES and shaders. Keep in mind, OpenGL ES version 1 runs on fixed-function piplelines, while OpenGL ES 2/3 runs on shaders.

Fixed-Function Pipelines

Older devices will have hardware that employs a fixed-function pipeline. In these older GPUs, there was specific dedicated hardware for perform functions. Functions, such as transformations, were performed by dedicated parts of the GPU that you, as a developer, had little to no control over. This means that you would simply hand your vertices to the GPU, tell it to transform the vertices, and that's it.

An example of a transformation can be when you have a set of vertices representing a cube, and you want to move that cube from one location to another. This would be accomplished by putting the vertices into the fixed-function pipeline, and then telling the hardware to perform a transformation on those vertices. The hardware would then do the matrix math for you and determine the placement of the final cube.

In the following code, you will see a very simplified version of what you would do in a fixed-function pipeline. The vertices myVertices are sent into the pipeline. The glTranslatef() is then used to translate the vertices to new positions. The ensuing matrix math is done for you in the GPU.

```
private float myVertices[] = {
0.0f, 0.0f, 0.0f,
   1.0f, 0.0f, 0.0f,
   1.0f, 1.0f, 0.0f,
   0.0f, 1.0f, 0.0f,
};

//Other OpenGL and game stuff//

gl.glMatrixMode(GL10.GL_MODELVIEW)
gl.glLoadIdentity();
gl.glTranslatef(0f, 1f, 0f);
```

The advantage of this was that in using dedicated hardware, the function could be performed very quickly. Hardware can perform functions at very fast rates, and dedicated hardware—or hardware that has a very limited function set—can perform functions even faster.

The disadvantage to this fixed-function pipeline approach is that hardware cannot be changed or reconfigured like software can. This limits the usefulness of the hardware moving forward. Also, specialized hardware can only perform functions on one queue item at a time. This means that the pipeline can often be slowed down if there are a great amount of items waiting in the queue to be processed.

Newer devices, on the other hand, have GPUs that use shaders. A shader is still a specialized piece of hardware, but it is much more flexible than its fixed-function predecessor. OpenGL ES works with shaders by using a programming language called GLSL or OpenGL Shading Language to perform any number of programmable tasks.

Shaders

A shader is a software program, written in a shader language, that performs all of the functionality that used to be handled by the fixed-function hardware. OpenGL ES 2 / 3 works with two different types of shaders: vertex shaders and fragment shaders.

Vertex Shaders

A vertex shader performs functions on vertices, such as transforming the color, position, and texture of the vertex. The shader will run on every vertex passed into it. This means that if you have a shape made from 256 vertices, the vertex shader will run on each one of them.

Vertices can be small or large. However, in all cases, vertices will consist of many pixels. The vertex shader will work on all of the pixels in a single vertex the same way. All of the pixels within a single vertex are treated as a single entity. When the vertex shader is finished, it passes the vertex downstream to the rasterizer, and then on to the fragment shader.

Following is a basic vertex shader:

```
private final String vertexShaderCode =
        "uniform mat4 uMVPMatrix;" +
        "attribute vec4 vPosition;" +
        "attribute vec2 TexCoordIn;" +
        "varying vec2 TexCoordOut;" +
        "void main() {" +
        "  gl_Position = uMVPMatrix * vPosition;" +
        "  TexCoordOut = TexCoordIn;" +
        "}";
```

Fragment Shaders

Whereas vertex shaders process data for an entire vertex, fragment shaders—sometimes known as pixel shaders—work on each pixel. The fragment shader will make computations for lighting, shading, fog, color, and other things that would affect single pixels within a vertex. Processes for gradients and lighting are performed on the pixel level because they can be applied differently across a vertex.

Following is a basic fragment shader:

```
private final String fragmentShaderCode =
        "precision mediump float;" +
        "uniform vec4 vColor;" +
        "uniform sampler2D TexCoordIn;" +
        "varying vec2 TexCoordOut;" +
        "void main() {" +
        "  gl_FragColor = texture2D(TexCoordIn, TexCoordOut);" +
        "}";
```

> **Note**   There are other types of shaders including Tessellation shaders and Geometry shaders. These can be optional and are handled within the hardware. You will have little to no awareness into their operation.

Most Android devices now can handle a combination of OpenGL ES 1 and OpenGL ES 2 calls. Some developers, if they are uncomfortable with programming shaders, will continue to use fixed-function pipeline calls for the viewport and other dynamics. Be aware that as OpenGL progresses, compatibility with the fixed-function pipeline calls of OpenGL ES is being phased out. There will be a time in the very near future when you will be forced to use only shaders within OpenGL ES. Therefore, if you are at an early point in your career with OpenGL ES, I would suggest making an earnest effort to use shaders whenever possible.

How Games Work

When developing a game or a game loop, the code needs to be executed in a certain order, at certain times. Knowing this execution flow is crucial in understanding how your code should be set up.

The following sections will outline a basic game flow or game loop.

A Basic Game Loop

At the core of every video game is the game engine, and part of that game engine is the game loop. As the name suggests, the game engine is the code that powers the game. Every game, regardless of the type of game—whether it is an RPG, a first-person shooter, a platformer, or even an RTS—requires a fully featured game engine to run.

The game engine typically runs on its own thread, giving it as many resources as possible. All of the tasks that a game needs to run, from graphics to sound, are taken care of in the game engine.

> **Note**   The engine of any one game is purposely built to be generic. This allows it to be used and reused in multiple situations, possibly for different games.

One very popular multipurpose game engine is the Unreal engine. The Unreal engine, first developed around 1998 by Epic for its first-person shooter, Unreal, has been used in hundreds of games. The Unreal engine is easily adaptable and works with a variety of game types, not just first-person shooters. This generic structure and flexibility make the Unreal engine popular with not only professions but casual developers as well.

Chances are, in your game development, you might have used a third-party game engine. There are many free and fee-based ones available for Android. This book will be of far greater help to you, though, if you are looking to build your own game engine.

Many of the processes in third-party game engines become obfuscated, and you might not have access to the debugging capability or you might not be able to modify the code within the engine.

When you have a problem, you will generally have to turn to the company that developed the engine, and it could take time for the original developer to fix it—if they even fix it at all. This can be a major drawback if you are thinking about using a third-party game engine.

There is no substitute for the experience of building your own game engine. This book assumes that you are doing just that. Many of the problems that will be tackled in the rest of this book assume you are attempting to write a game engine on Android and are running into some common problems.

So what exactly does the game engine do? The game engine handles all of the grunt work of the game execution, anything from playing the sound effects and background music to rendering graphics onto the screen. The following is a partial list of the functions that a typical game engine will perform.

- Graphics rendering
- Animation
- Sound
- Collision detection
- Artificial intelligence (AI)
- Physics (non-collision)
- Threading and memory management
- Networking
- Command interpreter (IO)

At the core of the game engine is the game loop. While the engine can handle anything from setting up one-time vertices buffers and retrieving images, the game loop serves up the actual code execution of the game.

All games are executed in a code loop. The faster this loop can execute, the better the game will run, the quicker it will react to the player, and the smoother the action will appear on the screen. All of the code necessary to build drawing on the screen, move the game objects, tally the score, detect the collisions, and validate or invalidate items is executed within the game loop.

A game loop is exactly that, a group of code that is executed on a continuous loop. The loop is started when the game begins, and does not stop executing—with some exceptions—until the game is stopped. Let's take a look at all of the things a game loop can be expected to do on every one of its iterations. A typical game loop can do the following:

- Interpret the commands of an input device
- Track the characters and/or the background to make sure none move where they should not be able to move to
- Test for collisions between objects
- Move the background as needed
- Draw a background

- Draw any number of stationary items

- Calculate the physics of any mobile objects

- Move any weapons/bullets/items that have been repositioned

- Draw weapons/bullets/items

- Move the characters independently

- Draw the characters

- Play sound effects

- Spin off threads for continuous background music

- Track the player's score

- Track and manage networked or multiple players

This is not be a comprehensive list, but it is a fairly good list of all of the things expected to be done within the game loop.

It is very important to refine and optimize all of your game code. The more optimized you can make your code in the game loop, the faster it will execute all of the calls it needs to make, thus giving you the best possible gaming experience. In the next section, we will take a look at how Android, as a platform, handles game engines and game loops.

Android and Game Engines

Android is packaged with a powerful, fully featured graphics API called OpenGL ES. But is OpenGL ES absolutely necessary for game development? Rather than go through the trouble of learning a fairly low-level API, such as OpenGL ES, can you just write a game with core Android API calls?

The short answer is that for a game to run efficiently, it cannot rely on the core Android API calls to do this kind of heavy duty work. Yes, most Android does have core calls that could take care of every item on this list. However, the rendering, sound, and memory systems of Android are built for generic tasks and adapt to any number of unpredictable uses, without specializing in any one. Unpredictability means one thing: overhead. The core Android API calls that could take care of the jobs needed to run a game come with a lot of extraneous code. This is acceptable if you are writing business applications, but not if you are writing games. Overhead adds slowness to your code, and games require something with a little more power.

For a game to run smoothly and quickly, the code will need to bypass the overhead that is inherent in core Android API calls; that is, a game should communicate directly with the graphics hardware to perform graphics function, communicate directly with the sound card to play sound effects, and so on. If you were to use the standard memory, graphics, and sound systems that are available to you through core Android API, your game could be threaded with all of the other Android applications that are running on the system. This would make for a choppy looking game that would run very slowly.

For this reason, game engines and game loops are almost always coded in low-level languages or specific API, such as OpenGL ES. As we will touch on in Chapter 2, low-level languages offer a more direct path to the hardware of the system. A game engine needs to be able to take code and commands from the engine and pass them directly to the hardware. This allows the game to run quickly and with all of the control that it needs to be able to provide a rewarding experience.

Summary

In this chapter, we covered what tools you will need to get the most out of this book. Android version Jelly Bean, Eclipse Kepler, and some basic Java and/or game development experience will help you throughout the remainder of this book. We also covered the differences between OpenGL ES versions 1 and 2 / 3, and the difference between fixed pipelines and shaders.

In the next few chapters, we will begin to look at some of the problems in a typical game engine. More specifically, we will look at the problems that could occur with the different ways to load an image. There are many different image formats and a handful of different ways to load these images and display them to the screen. Chances are, if you have tried, you have run into some pretty unexpected results.

Chapter **2**

Loading an Image

It should go without saying that if you plan on developing a game, casual or otherwise, you need to work with images. Everything from the backgrounds and characters to the menus and text is made up of images. Android can use different methods to serve up these images to the screen. This chapter will help to solve any problems that you have had retrieving, storing, and serving images within Android.

There are two distinct ways to serve up an image in Android, and each has its place in game development. The first way to serve up an image in Android is to use core Android methods—or those methods that do not involve the direct use of OpenGL ES. These core methods require little to no code to use, but they are slow and definitely not flexible enough to be used in the main, action-oriented parts of the game.

The second way to serve up images within Android is to use OpenGL ES. OpenGL ES is fast, flexible, and perfect for use within a game; however, it requires substantially more code than the core Android methods do. We will look at both of these in this chapter.

So when would you use one method over the other?

Images loaded using the core Android methods are perfect for splash screens, title screens, and even menus. Given the architecture of Android activities, it is very easy to create an activity using core Android methods, that contains a menu system for the game. Menus can include items that are easier accomplished before launching your game thread, such as checking scores, visiting an online shop, or viewing preloaded level information. The menu can then be used to launch the main game thread when the player chooses to enter the game. Once in the main game thread, OpenGL ES can take over the duties of working with the more graphic-intense gameplay. The solutions in this chapter will help you work around many common problems loading images in both OpenGL ES and using core Android methods.

2.1 Loading an Image Using Core Android Methods

Problem

There are times in a game when you might not need to use OpenGL ES for displaying images; for example, the title and menu screens. However, after you have decided to use either core Android methods or OpenGL ES, how do you store the images in your project so that Android can access them?

Solution

Image files are stored in the res folder prior to being used within Android. The res folder—or resource folder—is where all of the resources for your Android project are stored. There is a set of subdirectories for the res folder named drawable*. All of your images should be placed in a drawable folder. The Android ImageView node is then used to display these images to the screen. This is a perfect solution for game splash screens or any part of your game that displays an image before the actual gameplay starts.

How It Works

One of the good things about this solution is that it can be accomplished with no manual coding whatsoever. Some drag-and-drop action will set this solution up for you in an instant. Since this solution has two parts (storing and displaying images), let's take a look at each part separately.

Storing Imagesin Android

The first part of the problem is where you store images for use within Android. All of the resource files that you use in your Android projects are kept in a project directory named res. If you open your project, and expand the file system under the Project Explorer, you will see a root level folder named res; this is where all of your in-app resources, such as strings and images, are stored.

> **Note**   If you are using Eclipse (the latest version as of the writing of this book is Juno) then you will see the res folder in the Package Explorer. However, if you are using a different IDE, or no IDE at all, then locate the file exploring equivalent to see the res folder.

If you are using an IDE, open the res folder and you should find a number of subfolders. Some of these subfolders should start with the word drawable-. All of the subfolders that are meant for storing images within your app will start with this word. You will also notice a notation at the end of the name of each folder, from -ldpi to -xhdpi. What does this mean?

Android supports a number of different screen sizes and pixel densities. Because you might want to have different resolution images for different screen sizes or pixel densities, Android provides different subfolders for these images. The notation in the folder name indicates screen size from small (drawable-small)to extra large(drawable-xlarge), and indicates pixel densities from low density(drawable-ldpi) to extra-high density(drawable-xhdpi).

> **Tip**   If you do not care about the pixel density of the screen used to display your images, then you can put all of your files in the default drawable folder. If your IDE did not create this folder by default, feel free to add it. Android will look here when you have not specified a pixel density to use.

The image that we will use in this example is the splash screen to our fictitious game Super Bandit Guy, as shown in Figure 2-1.

Figure 2-1. Super Bandit Guy splash screen image

Simply drag and drop this image from your working folder, wherever that may be, to the correct drawable dpi folder, as shown in Figure 2-2. In this case, I used the drawable-xhdpi to test on a tablet.

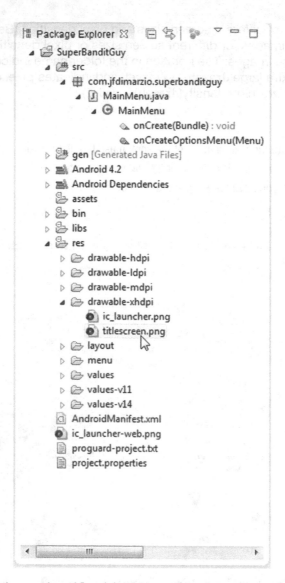

Figure 2-2. Dragging an image to the `res/drawable-xhdpi` *folder*

That is all there is to getting the image into Android.

> **Caution**   All image files names must begin with a lowercase letter to be used in Android.

Loading and Displaying Images

The image is now ready to use. To display this image to the screen, you need to create an ImageView.

> **Note**   Again, if you are using Eclipse, a generic layout should have been created for you just for this purpose. If you are not using Eclipse, please follow your IDE's instructions for creating a *main screen layout*.

Expand the layout root folder, and open the `activity_main_menu.xml` file. With the layout open, expand the Images & Media palette and locate the ImageView, as shown in Figure 2-3.

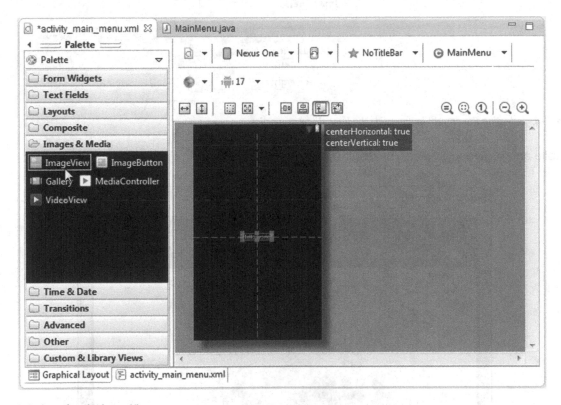

Figure 2-3. Locating the ImageView

Now drag the image from the palette to the layout in the work area. At the top of the working area (again reference Figure 2-3), you will see a row of menu icons. Selecting the state menu icon will allow you to change the orientation of the screen layout from portrait to landscape. I have seen games played in either orientation; however, for this example, Super Bandit Guy is played in landscape. Therefore, a change in orientation will be noticeable in future screen shots.With the ImageView added to your layout, expand the ImageView properties and select the Src property. Clicking on the ellipsis next to the Src property will bring up a list of drawable resources.

Select the correct image, as shown in Figure 2-4.

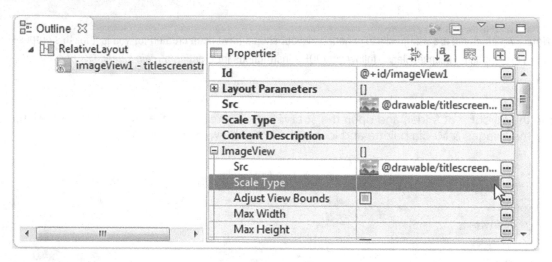

Figure 2-4. Selecting the correct image using the ImageView properties

Compile and run your project. The result should appear as shown in Figure 2-5.

Figure 2-5. Displaying the splash image

There is one piece of business that you might want to take care of before calling this one finished. Notice in Figure 2-5 that there is an action bar menu above the image. This is added by default (in Android version 3.0 and higher) in some IDEs depending on the Android theme that is selected when creating your project. Getting rid of this action bar is easy.

Returning to the Project Explorer, within the res folder, you should be able to locate a folder named values. Inside this folder is a file named styles.xml. Add the following line to the styles.xml file, between the style tags of the style that your app is using.

```
<item name="android:windowActionBar">false</item>
```

2.2 Loading an Image Using OpenGL ES

In this recipe, I present two problems and two solutions. You'll first correct ImageView image calls to run properly in a game. Then you'll see how to ensure OpenGL ES displays the correct image when using an Android device.

Problem 1

ImageView image calls are too slow for use in a game.

Solution 1

Use OpenGL ES to write your images to the screen. You must create an OpenGL ES renderer, a GLSurfaceView, and a set of vertices and textures. Although this solution might sound like a lot of work, you will only need to do much of the work once, and then you can reuse the same classes throughout your project.

That is, the renderer and the GLSurfaceView need to be created only once for your game. They are reused over and over again. The only parts of the solution that you will need to re-create for every image you want to display are the vertices and textures that define the image.

How It Works

We are going to break this solution up into three parts: creating the vertices and textures, creating the renderer, and finally creating the GLSurfaceView. Let's start with creating the vertices and textures.

Create Vertices and Textures

This is the most complicated part of the process, and the one that requires the most code. But if you take it slow, it should be no problem. Also, given that creating the vertices and textures is the one part that will be repeated throughout your game in some form, you will get a lot of practice with the code. It will get easier the more you use it.

As far as OpenGL ES is concerned, all images are textures. Textures are meant to be mapped onto a shape. You will be creating a primitive square to map your image (or texture) onto and display it to the screen through the renderer and the GLSurfaceView.

To do so, you need to create a new class, SBGSplash, which involves the following steps, all of which will be described shortly:

1. Create some buffers.

2. Create the constructor.

3. Create the loadTexture() method.

4. Create the draw() method.

The constructor for the SBGSplash class is going to set up all of the variables that you need to interact with OpenGL ES (see Listing 2-1). You need an array to hold the mapping coordinates of your texture, an array to hold the coordinates of your vertices, and an array to hold the indices of the vertices. Finally, you create an array of resource identifiers that refer to your textures.

Listing 2-1. SBGSplash (OpenGL ES 1)

```
public class SBGSplash {
private int[] textures = new int[1];

private float[]vertices = {
0f, 1f, 0f,
0f, 0f, 0f,
1f, 0f, 0f,
1f, 1f, 0f,
};
private float[] texture = {
1f, 0f,
1f, 1f,
0f, 1f,
0f, 0f,
};
private byte[] indices = {
0,1,2,
0,2,3,
};
public SBGSplash() {
//empty constructor
}
}
```

The textures array holds an identifier to each texture that you are loading. You are hard-coding this to 1 because you will only be loading one image, but we are leaving this flexible enough for you to reuse in the future without much rewriting.

The vertices array lists a series of points. Each row here represents the x, y, and z value of a corner of a square. This square is the primitive shape that the image will be textured to in order to be displayed. In this case, you are making a square that is the full size of the screen, ensuring that the image covers the entire screen.

The texture array represents where the corners of the image (or texture) will line up with the corners of the square you created. Again, in this case, you want the texture to cover the entire square, which in turn is covering the entire background.

Finally, the indices array holds the definition for the face of the square. The face of the square is broken into two triangles. The values in this array are the corners of those triangles in counterclockwise order. Notice that one line (two points) overlap (0 and 3).

If you are using OpenGL ES 3, you need to add your shader code here, as shown in Listing 2-2.

Listing 2-2. SBGSplash (OpenGL ES 2/3)

```java
public class SBGSplash {
private final String vertexShaderCode =
"uniform mat4 uMVPMatrix;" +
"attribute vec4 vPosition;" +
"attribute vec2 TexCoordIn;" +
"varying vec2 TexCoordOut;" +
"void main() {" +
"  gl_Position = uMVPMatrix * vPosition;" +
"  TexCoordOut = TexCoordIn;" +
"}";
private final String fragmentShaderCode =
"precision mediump float;" +
"uniform vec4 vColor;" +
"uniform sampler2D TexCoordIn;" +
"uniform float scroll;" +
"varying vec2 TexCoordOut;" +
"void main() {" +
" gl_FragColor = texture2D(TexCoordIn, vec2(TexCoordOut.x + scroll,TexCoordOut.y));"+
"}";
private int[] textures = new int[1];

private float[]vertices = {
0f, 1f, 0f,
0f, 0f, 0f,
1f, 0f, 0f,
1f, 1f, 0f,
};
private float[] texture = {
1f, 0f,
1f, 1f,
0f, 1f,
0f, 0f,
};
private byte[] indices = {
0,1,2,
0,2,3,
};
public SBGSplash() {
//empty constructor
}
}
```

It is time to create the buffers that are also used in the class constructor. Because the buffers, like the variables in the previous code listing, are used in multiple methods in the class, we will set them up in the body of the class.

Create Buffers

Now, create some buffers that we can use to hold these arrays (see Listing 2-3). The buffers are what will then be loaded into OpenGL ES 1.

Listing 2-3. Buffers (OpenGL ES 1)

```
importjava.nio.ByteBuffer;
importjava.nio.FloatBuffer;

public class SBGSplash {

private FloatBuffervertexBuffer;
private FloatBuffertextureBuffer;
private ByteBufferindexBuffer;

private int[] textures = new int[1];

private float[]vertices = {
0f, 1f, 0f,
0f, 0f, 0f,
1f, 0f, 0f,
1f, 1f, 0f,
};
private float[] texture = {
1f, 0f,
1f, 1f,
0f, 1f,
0f, 0f,
};
private byte[] indices = {
0,1,2,
0,2,3,
};
public SBGSplash() {
}
}
```

OpenGL ES 2 and 3 require a few extra variables with the buffers, as show in Listing 2-4.

Listing 2-4. Buffers and Variables (OpenGL ES 2/3)

```
public class SBGSplash {
private final FloatBuffer vertexBuffer;
private final ShortBuffer indexBuffer;
private final FloatBuffer textureBuffer;
```

```
private final int mProgram;
private int mPositionHandle;
private int mMVPMatrixHandle;

static final int COORDS_PER_VERTEX = 3;
static final int COORDS_PER_TEXTURE = 2;
private final int vertexStride = COORDS_PER_VERTEX * 4;
public static int textureStride = COORDS_PER_TEXTURE * 4;
private final String vertexShaderCode =
"uniform mat4 uMVPMatrix;" +
"attribute vec4 vPosition;" +
"attribute vec2 TexCoordIn;" +
"varying vec2 TexCoordOut;" +
"void main() {" +
"  gl_Position = uMVPMatrix * vPosition;" +
"  TexCoordOut = TexCoordIn;" +
"}";
private final String fragmentShaderCode =
"precision mediump float;" +
"uniform vec4 vColor;" +
"uniform sampler2D TexCoordIn;" +
"uniform float scroll;" +
"varying vec2 TexCoordOut;" +
"void main() {" +
" gl_FragColor = texture2D(TexCoordIn, vec2(TexCoordOut.x + scroll,TexCoordOut.y));"+
"}";
private int[] textures = new int[1];

private float[]vertices = {
0f, 1f, 0f,
0f, 0f, 0f,
1f, 0f, 0f,
1f, 1f, 0f,
};
private float[] texture = {
1f, 0f,
1f, 1f,
0f, 1f,
0f, 0f,
};
private byte[] indices = {
0,1,2,
 0,2,3,
};
public SBGSplash() {
//empty constructor
}
}
```

The buffers are filled in the class's constructor. Right now, the constructor is empty. The next section describes what code is needed to complete the constructor.

Create the Constructor

Now populate the appropriate buffers with the appropriate arrays in the SBGSplash constructor, as shown in Listings 2-5 and 2-6.

Listing 2-5. Constructor (OpenGL ES 1)

```
import java.nio.ByteOrder;
import java.nio.ByteBuffer;
import java.nio.FloatBuffer;

public class SBGSplash {

...

public SBGSplash() {

ByteBufferbyteBuf = ByteBuffer.allocateDirect(vertices.length * 4);
byteBuf.order(ByteOrder.nativeOrder());
vertexBuffer = byteBuf.asFloatBuffer();
vertexBuffer.put(vertices);
vertexBuffer.position(0);

byteBuf = ByteBuffer.allocateDirect(texture.length * 4);
byteBuf.order(ByteOrder.nativeOrder());
textureBuffer = byteBuf.asFloatBuffer();
textureBuffer.put(texture);
textureBuffer.position(0);

indexBuffer = ByteBuffer.allocateDirect(indices.length);
indexBuffer.order(ByteOrder.nativeOrder());
indexBuffer.put(indices);
indexBuffer.position(0);
}
}
```

Listing 2-6. Constructor (OpenGL ES 2/3)

```
public class SBGSplash {

...

public SBGSplash() {

ByteBuffer byteBuf = ByteBuffer.allocateDirect(vertices.length * 4);
byteBuf.order(ByteOrder.nativeOrder());
vertexBuffer = byteBuf.asFloatBuffer();
vertexBuffer.put(vertices);
vertexBuffer.position(0);
```

```
byteBuf = ByteBuffer.allocateDirect(texture.length * 4);
byteBuf.order(ByteOrder.nativeOrder());
textureBuffer = byteBuf.asFloatBuffer();
textureBuffer.put(texture);
textureBuffer.position(0);

indexBuffer = ByteBuffer.allocateDirect(indices.length);
indexBuffer.order(ByteOrder.nativeOrder());
indexBuffer.put(indices);
indexBuffer.position(0);

int vertexShader = GLES20.glCreateShader(GLES20.GL_VERTEX_SHADER);
GLES20.glShaderSource(vertexShader, vertexShaderCode);
GLES20.glCompileShader(vertexShader);

int fragmentShader = GLES20.glCreateShader(GLES20.GL_FRAGMENT_SHADER);
GLES20.glShaderSource(fragmentShader, fragmentShaderCode);
GLES20.glCompileShader(fragmentShader);

mProgram = GLES20.glCreateProgram();
GLES20.glAttachShader(mProgram, vertexShader);
GLES20.glAttachShader(mProgram, fragmentShader);
GLES20.glLinkProgram(mProgram);
}
}
```

The code here should be pretty self-explanatory. You are creating a `ByteBuffer` with the values of the vertex and texture arrays. Notice that the number of values in each of these arrays is multiplied by 4 to allocate space in the `ByteBuffer`. This is because the values in the arrays are floats, and floats are 4 times the size of bytes. The index array is integers and it can be loaded directly into the `indexBuffer`.

The only difference between the OpenGL ES 1 code and the OpenGL ES 2/3 code is that OpenGL ES 2/3 requires that the shaders be attached to the program. Three lines of code compile each shader and attach it to the program.

Create the `loadTexture()` Method

Next, you need to create the `loadTexture()` method (see Listings 2-7 and 2-8). The `loadTexture()` method will take in an image identifier and then load the image into a stream. The stream will then be loaded as a texture into OpenGL ES. During the drawing process you will map this texture onto the vertices.

Listing 2-7. loadTexture() (OpenGL ES 1)

```java
public class SBGSplash {

...

public SBGSplash() {
...

}

public void loadTexture(GL10 gl,int texture, Context context) {
InputStreamimagestream = context.getResources().openRawResource(texture);
      Bitmap bitmap = null;
android.graphics.Matrix flip = new android.graphics.Matrix();
flip.postScale(-1f, -1f);
try {

bitmap = BitmapFactory.decodeStream(imagestream);

}catch(Exception e){
//handle your exception here
}finally {
//Always clear and close
try {
imagestream.close();
imagestream = null;
} catch (IOException e) {
}
}

gl.glGenTextures(1, textures, 0);
gl.glBindTexture(GL10.GL_TEXTURE_2D, textures[0]);

gl.glTexParameterf(GL10.GL_TEXTURE_2D, GL10.GL_TEXTURE_MIN_FILTER, GL10.GL_NEAREST);
gl.glTexParameterf(GL10.GL_TEXTURE_2D, GL10.GL_TEXTURE_MAG_FILTER, GL10.GL_LINEAR);

GLUtils.texImage2D(GL10.GL_TEXTURE_2D, 0, bitmap, 0);

bitmap.recycle();
    }

}
```

Listing 2-8. loadTexture() (OpenGL ES 2/3)

```
public class SBGSplash {

...

public SBGSplash() {
...

}

public void loadTexture(int texture, Context context) {
InputStream imagestream = context.getResources().openRawResource(texture);
Bitmap bitmap = null;

android.graphics.Matrix flip = new android.graphics.Matrix();
flip.postScale(-1f, -1f);

try {

bitmap = BitmapFactory.decodeStream(imagestream);
imagestream.close();
imagestream = null;

}catch(Exception e){

//handle your exception here

}

GLES20.glGenTextures(1, textures, 0);
GLES20.glBindTexture(GLES20.GL_TEXTURE_2D, textures[0]);

GLES20.glTexParameterf(GLES20.GL_TEXTURE_2D, GLES20.GL_TEXTURE_MIN_FILTER, GLES20.GL_NEAREST);
GLES20.glTexParameterf(GLES20.GL_TEXTURE_2D, GLES20.GL_TEXTURE_MAG_FILTER, GLES20.GL_LINEAR);

GLES20.glTexParameterf(GLES20.GL_TEXTURE_2D, GLES20.GL_TEXTURE_WRAP_S, GLES20.GL_REPEAT);
GLES20.glTexParameterf(GLES20.GL_TEXTURE_2D, GLES20.GL_TEXTURE_WRAP_T, GLES20.GL_REPEAT);

GLUtils.texImage2D(GLES20.GL_TEXTURE_2D, 0, bitmap, 0);

bitmap.recycle();

    }

}
```

The first part of loadTexture() is pretty easy. It takes in the identifier and loads the resulting image into a bitmap stream. The texture that is passed into openRawResource() is the resource ID for an image in your res folder. You will pass this later in the solution. The stream is then closed. Also, because OpenGL ES displays images in a first in/last out byte order, by default images will appear upside down. Therefore, you use a Matrix to flip the image by calling postScale().

The second part of loadTexture(), however, is fairly heavy in OpenGL ES. The first line generates a texture pointer. This pointer is structured like a dictionary.

```
gl.glGenTextures(1, textures, 0);
...
GLES20.glGenTextures(1, textures, 0);
```

The first parameter is the number of texture names that you need generated. When it comes time to bind the textures to a set of vertices, you will call them out of OpenGL ES by name. Here, you are only loading one texture; therefore, you need only one texture name generated. The second parameter is the array of int that you created to hold the number for each texture. Again, there is only one value in this array right now. Finally, the last parameter holds the offset for the pointer into the array. Because your array is 0-based, the offset is 0.

The second line binds the texture into OpenGL ES.

```
gl.glBindTexture(GL10.GL_TEXTURE_2D, textures[0]);
...
GLES20.glBindTexture(GLES20.GL_TEXTURE_2D, textures[0]);
```

If you were to have two textures that you were loading together, you would have two each of these first two lines—one to load the first image and one to load the second.

The next two lines deal with how OpenGL is to map the texture onto the vertices. You want the mapping to take place quickly, but produce sharpened pixels.

```
gl.glTexParameterf(GL10.GL_TEXTURE_2D, GL10.GL_TEXTURE_MIN_FILTER, GL10.GL_NEAREST);
gl.glTexParameterf(GL10.GL_TEXTURE_2D, GL10.GL_TEXTURE_MAG_FILTER, GL10.GL_LINEAR);
...
GLES20.glTexParameterf(GLES20.GL_TEXTURE_2D, GLES20.GL_TEXTURE_MIN_FILTER, GLES20.GL_NEAREST);
GLES20.glTexParameterf(GLES20.GL_TEXTURE_2D, GLES20.GL_TEXTURE_MAG_FILTER, GLES20.GL_LINEAR);
```

Finally, in the last two lines of the loadTexture() method, you associate the bitmap input stream that you created with the number 1 texture. The bitmap stream is then recycled.

```
GLUtils.texImage2D(GL10.GL_TEXTURE_2D, 0, bitmap, 0);

bitmap.recycle();
...
GLUtils.texImage2D(GLES20.GL_TEXTURE_2D, 0, bitmap, 0);
bitmap.recycle();
```

Create the draw() Method

The last piece of code you need to write to complete your SBGSplash class is the method that will draw() the texture onto the vertices (Listings 2-9 and 2-10).

Listing 2-9. draw() (OpenGL ES 1)

```
...
public class SBGSplash {
...
public void draw(GL10 gl) {

gl.glBindTexture(GL10.GL_TEXTURE_2D, textures[0]);

gl.glFrontFace(GL10.GL_CCW);
gl.glEnable(GL10.GL_CULL_FACE);
gl.glCullFace(GL10.GL_BACK);

gl.glEnableClientState(GL10.GL_VERTEX_ARRAY);
gl.glEnableClientState(GL10.GL_TEXTURE_COORD_ARRAY);

gl.glVertexPointer(3, GL10.GL_FLOAT, 0, vertexBuffer);
gl.glTexCoordPointer(2, GL10.GL_FLOAT, 0, textureBuffer);

gl.glDrawElements(GL10.GL_TRIANGLES, indices.length, GL10.GL_UNSIGNED_BYTE, indexBuffer);

gl.glDisableClientState(GL10.GL_VERTEX_ARRAY);
gl.glDisableClientState(GL10.GL_TEXTURE_COORD_ARRAY);
gl.glDisable(GL10.GL_CULL_FACE);

}

public SBGSplash() {
...

}
public void loadTexture(GL10 gl,int texture, Context context) {
...
    }

}
```

Listing 2-10. draw() (OpenGL ES 2/3)

```
public class SBGSplash {
...
public void draw(GL10 gl) {
GLES20.glUseProgram(mProgram);

mPositionHandle = GLES20.glGetAttribLocation(mProgram, "vPosition");

GLES20.glEnableVertexAttribArray(mPositionHandle);

int vsTextureCoord = GLES20.glGetAttribLocation(mProgram, "TexCoordIn");
```

```
GLES20.glVertexAttribPointer(mPositionHandle, COORDS_PER_VERTEX,
GLES20.GL_FLOAT, false,
vertexStride, vertexBuffer);
GLES20.glVertexAttribPointer(vsTextureCoord, COORDS_PER_TEXTURE,
GLES20.GL_FLOAT, false,
textureStride, textureBuffer);
GLES20.glEnableVertexAttribArray(vsTextureCoord);
GLES20.glActiveTexture(GLES20.GL_TEXTURE0);
GLES20.glBindTexture(GLES20.GL_TEXTURE_2D, textures[0]);
int fsTexture = GLES20.glGetUniformLocation(mProgram, "TexCoordOut");
GLES20.glUniform1i(fsTexture, 0);

mMVPMatrixHandle = GLES20.glGetUniformLocation(mProgram, "uMVPMatrix");

GLES20.glUniformMatrix4fv(mMVPMatrixHandle, 1, false, mvpMatrix, 0);

GLES20.glDrawElements(GLES20.GL_TRIANGLES, drawOrder.length,
GLES20.GL_UNSIGNED_SHORT, drawListBuffer);

GLES20.glDisableVertexAttribArray(mPositionHandle);

}

public SBGSplash() {
...

}
public void loadTexture(GL10 gl,int texture, Context context) {
...
    }

}
```

The draw() method is going to be called every time you want to draw this image to the screen, as opposed to the loadTexture() method, which will only be called when you initialize the game.

This first line of this method binds the texture to your target. The texture is loaded up and ready to be used.

```
gl.glBindTexture(GL10.GL_TEXTURE_2D, textures[0]);
```

The next three lines in the draw() method tell OpenGL ES to enable culling and basically not deal with any vertices that are not on the front face. Because you are rendering the game in 2D orthogonal view, you don't want OpenGL ES to spend precious processor time dealing with vertices that the player will never see. Right now, all of your vertices are front facing, but this is good code to have in there anyway.

```
gl.glFrontFace(GL10.GL_CCW);
gl.glEnable(GL10.GL_CULL_FACE);
gl.glCullFace(GL10.GL_BACK);
```

The next four lines enable the vertex and texture states, and then the vertices and texture buffers are loaded into OpenGL ES.

```
gl.glEnableClientState(GL10.GL_VERTEX_ARRAY);
gl.glEnableClientState(GL10.GL_TEXTURE_COORD_ARRAY);
gl.glVertexPointer(3, GL10.GL_FLOAT, 0, vertexBuffer);
gl.glTexCoordPointer(2, GL10.GL_FLOAT, 0, textureBuffer);
```

Finally, the texture is drawn onto the vertices, and the all of the states that were enabled are disabled.

```
gl.glDrawElements(GL10.GL_TRIANGLES, indices.length, GL10.GL_UNSIGNED_BYTE, indexBuffer);
gl.glDisableClientState(GL10.GL_VERTEX_ARRAY);
gl.glDisableClientState(GL10.GL_TEXTURE_COORD_ARRAY);
gl.glDisable(GL10.GL_CULL_FACE);
```

The SBGSplash class is now finished. All you need to do is create the supporting classes that will aid in displaying SBGSplash to the screen. This is done via the render.

Create the Renderer

Create a new class, SBGGameRenderer.

```
public class SBGGameRenderer{

}
```

Now you need to implement the GLSurfaceView's Renderer.

```
importandroid.opengl.GLSurfaceView.Renderer;
```

```
public class SBGGameRenderer implements Renderer{

}
```

Be sure to add in the unimplemented methods.

Listing 2-11. SBGGameRenderer()

```
importjavax.microedition.khronos.egl.EGLConfig;
import javax.microedition.khronos.opengles.GL10;

importandroid.opengl.GLSurfaceView.Renderer;

public class SBGGameRenderer implements Renderer{

@Override
public void onDrawFrame(GL10 gl) {
//TODO Auto-generated method stub

}
```

```
@Override
public void onSurfaceChanged(GL10 gl, int width, int height) {

}

@Override
public void onSurfaceCreated(GL10 gl, EGLConfigconfig) {

}
}
```

The function of these methods should be fairly self-explanatory. The onSurfaceCreated() method is called when the GLSurface is created. The onSurfaceChanged() method is called when the size of the View has changed (including the initial load). Finally, the onDrawFrame() method is call when the Renderer draws a frame to the screen.

Let's start coding them in the order that they are called. First up is the onSurfaceCreated() method.

The onSurfaceCreated() Method

In the onSurfaceCreated() method, you are going to initialize your OpenGL ES and load your textures, as shown in Listing 2-12.

Listing 2-12. onSurfaceCreated()

```
public class SBGGameRenderer implements Renderer{

private SBGSplashsplashImage = new SBGSplash();

@Override
public void onDrawFrame(GL10 gl) {
}
@Override
public void onSurfaceChanged(GL10 gl, int width, int height) {
}

@Override
public void onSurfaceCreated(GL10 gl, EGLConfigconfig) {
gl.glEnable(GL10.GL_TEXTURE_2D);
}
}
```

Notice that the onSurfaceCreated() method takes an instance of OpenGL ES (GL10 gl) as a parameter. This will get passed into the method by the GLSurfaceView when the Renderer is called. It is only used if you are using OpenGL ES 1; otherwise, it is ignored. You do not have to worry about creating an instance of GL10 for this process; it will be done for you automatically.

Next, you want to tell OpenGL ES to test the depth of all of the objects in your surface. This will need some explaining. Even though you are creating a 2D game, you will need to think in 3D terms.

Imagine that the OpenGL ES environment is a stage. Everything that you want to draw in your game is an actor on this stage. Now, imagine that you are filming the actors as they move around on the stage. The resulting movie is a 2D representation of what is happening on the stage. If one actor moves in front of another actor, the actor in the back will not be visible on the film. However, if you are watching these actors live in a theater, depending on where you are sitting, you might still be able to see the actor in the back.

This is the same idea as to how OpenGL ES is working under the hood. Even though you are making a 2D game, OpenGL ES is going to treat everything as if it were a 3D object in 3D space. In fact, one of the only differences to developing in 2D and developing in 3D in OpenGL ES is how you tell OpenGL ES to render the final scene. Therefore, you need to be mindful of where your objects are placed in the 3D space to make sure they render properly as a 2D game. By enabling OpenGL ES depth testing next (see Listing 2-13), you give OpenGL ES a means by which to test your textures and determine how they should be rendered.

Listing 2-13. Depth test

```
public class SBGBameRenderer implements Renderer{

private SBGSplashsplashImage = new SBGSplash();

@Override
public void onDrawFrame(GL10 gl) {
}
@Override
public void onSurfaceChanged(GL10 gl, int width, int height) {
}

@Override
public void onSurfaceCreated(GL10 gl, EGLConfigconfig) {
gl.glEnable(GL10.GL_TEXTURE_2D);
gl.glClearDepthf(1.0f);
gl.glEnable(GL10.GL_DEPTH_TEST);
gl.glDepthFunc(GL10.GL_LEQUAL);

}
}
```

The two last lines of code that you will add to this method concern blending. The two bold lines of code in Listing 2-14 will set OpenGL's blending feature to create transparency.

Listing 2-14. Blending

```
import javax.microedition.khronos.egl.EGLConfig;
import javax.microedition.khronos.opengles.GL10;
import android.opengl.GLSurfaceView.Renderer;

public class SBGGameRenderer implements Renderer{

private SBGSplashsplashImage = new SBGSplash();
```

```
@Override
public void onDrawFrame(GL10 gl) {
}
@Override
public void onSurfaceChanged(GL10 gl, int width, int height) {
}

@Override
public void onSurfaceCreated(GL10 gl, EGLConfigconfig) {
gl.glEnable(GL10.GL_TEXTURE_2D);
gl.glClearDepthf(1.0f);
gl.glEnable(GL10.GL_DEPTH_TEST);
gl.glDepthFunc(GL10.GL_LEQUAL);

gl.glEnable(GL10.GL_BLEND);
gl.glBlendFunc(GL10.GL_ONE, GL10.GL_ONE);
}
}
```

The next thing you should do in the onSurfaceCreated() method is load your textures. Call SGBSplash's loadTexture() in the onSurfaceChanged() method. Pass the loadTexture() method the resource identifier of the image you want to load. In Listing 2-15, I am using an image in the res/drawable folder named titlescreen.

Listing 2-15. onSurfaceCreated

```
public class SBGGameRenderer implements Renderer{
private SBGSplashsplashImage = new SBGSplash();

@Override
public void onDrawFrame(GL10 gl) {
}
@Override
public void onSurfaceChanged(GL10 gl, int width, int height) {
}

@Override
public void onSurfaceCreated(GL10 gl, EGLConfigconfig) {
gl.glEnable(GL10.GL_TEXTURE_2D);
gl.glClearDepthf(1.0f);
gl.glEnable(GL10.GL_DEPTH_TEST);
gl.glDepthFunc(GL10.GL_LEQUAL);

gl.glEnable(GL10.GL_BLEND);
gl.glBlendFunc(GL10.GL_ONE, GL10.GL_ONE);

splashImage.loadTexture(gl, R.drawable.titlescreen, context);
}
}
```

Notice that the loadTexture() method takes a context argument. Let's modify the constructor for SBGGameRenderer to allow for the passing of the application's context (see Listing 2-16). When the renderer is initiated, the context can be passed into the constructor and used throughout.

Listing 2-16. Modified constructor

```
public class SBGGameRenderer implements Renderer{

private SBGSplashsplashImage = new SBGSplash();

private Context context;

public SBGGameRenderer(Context appContext){
context = appContext;
}

@Override
public void onDrawFrame(GL10 gl) {
}
@Override
public void onSurfaceChanged(GL10 gl, int width, int height) {
}

@Override
public void onSurfaceCreated(GL10 gl, EGLConfigconfig) {
gl.glEnable(GL10.GL_TEXTURE_2D);
gl.glClearDepthf(1.0f);
gl.glEnable(GL10.GL_DEPTH_TEST);
gl.glDepthFunc(GL10.GL_LEQUAL);

gl.glEnable(GL10.GL_BLEND);
gl.glBlendFunc(GL10.GL_ONE, GL10.GL_ONE);

splashImage.loadTexture(gl, R.drawable.titlescreen, context);
}
}
```

The onSurfaceCreated() method for using OpenGL ES 2/3 is a bit lighter on code.

```
@Override
public void onSurfaceCreated(GL10 unused, EGLConfig config) {

GLES20.glClearColor(0.0f, 0.0f, 0.0f, 1.0f);

}
```

In OpenGL ES 2/3, the background color is being cleared out. This is really an optional step, as the entire screen area should be filled with game graphics anyway.

Now, let's move on to the onSurfaceChanged() method.

The onSurfacedChanged() Method

The onSurfacedChanged() method is going to handle all of the setup that is needed to display your images. Every time the screen is resized, the orientation is changed, and on the initial startup, this method is called.

You need to setup the glViewport() and then call the rendering routine to complete the onSurfacedChanged() method.

The glViewport() method takes four parameters. The first two parameters are the x and y coordinates of the lower left-hand corner of the screen. Typically, these values will be (0,0) because the lower left corner of the screen will be where the x and y axes meet; therefore, it is the 0 coordinate of each. The next two parameters of the glViewport() method are the width and the height of your viewport. Unless you want your game to be smaller than the device's screen, these should be set to the width and the height of the device. See Listing 2-17.

Listing 2-17. glViewport

```
public class SBGGameRenderer implements Renderer{

private SBGSplashsplashImage = new SBGSplash();

private Context context;

public SBGGameRenderer(Context appContext){
context = appContext;
}

@Override
public void onDrawFrame(GL10 gl) {
}
@Override
public void onSurfaceChanged(GL10 gl, int width, int height) {

gl.glViewport(0, 0, width,height);
}

@Override
public void onSurfaceCreated(GL10 gl, EGLConfigconfig) {

...

}
}
```

The calling GLSurfaceView will send in a width and height parameter to the onSurfacedChanged() method. You can simply set the width and the height of the glViewport() to the corresponding width and height sent in by the GLSurfaceView. See Listing 2-18.

Listing 2-18. width and height

```
public class SBGGameRenderer implements Renderer{

private SBGSplashsplashImage = new SBGSplash();

private Context context;

public SBGGameRenderer(Context appContext){
context = appContext;
}

@Override
public void onDrawFrame(GL10 gl) {
}
@Override
public void onSurfaceChanged(GL10 unused, int width, int height) {
GLES20.glViewport(0, 0, width, height);
float ratio = (float) width / height;
Matrix.frustumM(mProjMatrix, 0, -ratio, ratio, -1, 1, 3, 7);
}
@Override
public void onSurfaceCreated(GL10 gl, EGLConfigconfig) {

...

}
}
```

> **Note**   The width and height sent in by the GLSurfaceView will represent the width and height of the
> device minus the notification bar at the top of the screen.

If the glViewport() method represents the lens through which your scene is filmed, then the glOrthof() method is the image processor. With the viewport set, all you have to do now is use glOrthof() to render the surface.

To access glOrthof(), you need to put OpenGL ES 1 into projection matrix mode. OpenGL ES 1 has different matrix modes that let you access different parts of the stack. Throughout this book, you will access most, if not all, of them. This is the first one you will work with. Projection matrix mode gives you access to the way in which your scene is rendered.

To access projection matrix mode, you need to set the glMatrixMode() to GL_PROJECTION, as shown in Listing 2-19.

Listing 2-19. glMatrixMode

```java
public class SBGGameRenderer implements Renderer{

private SBGSplashsplashImage = new SBGSplash();

private Context context;

public SBGGameRenderer(Context appContext){
context = appContext;
}

@Override
public void onDrawFrame(GL10 gl) {
}
@Override
public void onSurfaceChanged(GL10 gl, int width, int height) {

gl.glViewport(0, 0, width, height);
gl.glMatrixMode(GL10.GL_PROJECTION);

}

@Override
public void onSurfaceCreated(GL10 gl, EGLConfigconfig) {

...

}
}
```

Now that OpenGL ES is in projection matrix mode, you need to load the current identity (see Listing 2-20). Think of the identity as the default state of OpenGL ES 1.

Listing 2-20. loading the identity

```java
public class SBGGameRenderer implements Renderer{

private SBGSplashsplashImage = new SBGSplash();

private Context context;

public SBGGameRenderer(Context appContext){
context = appContext;
}

@Override
public void onDrawFrame(GL10 gl) {
}
@Override
public void onSurfaceChanged(GL10 gl, int width, int height) {

gl.glViewport(0, 0, width, height);
```

```
gl.glMatrixMode(GL10.GL_PROJECTION);
gl.glLoadIdentity();

}

@Override
public void onSurfaceCreated(GL10 gl, EGLConfigconfig) {

...

}
}
```

Now that the identity is loaded, you can set up glOrthof()(see Listing 2-21).

Listing 2-21. glOrthof

```
public class SBGGameRenderer implements Renderer{

private SBGSplashsplashImage = new SBGSplash();

private Context context;

public SBGGameRenderer(Context appContext){
context = appContext;
}

@Override
public void onDrawFrame(GL10 gl) {
}
@Override

public void onSurfaceChanged(GL10 gl, int width, int height) {

gl.glViewport(0, 0, width,height);

gl.glMatrixMode(GL10.GL_PROJECTION);
gl.glLoadIdentity();
gl.glOrthof(0f, 1f, 0f, 1f, -1f, 1f);

}

@Override
public void onSurfaceCreated(GL10 gl, EGLConfigconfig) {

...

}
}
```

The glOrthof() method is going to set up an orthogonal, two-dimensional rendering of your scene. This call takes six parameters, each of which defines a clipping plane.

The clipping planes indicate to the renderer where to stop rendering. In other words, any images that fall outside of the clipping planes will not be picked up by glOrthof(). The six clipping planes are the left, right, bottom, top, near, and far. These represent points on the x, y, and z axes.

Now let's set up the onDraw() method.

The onDrawFrame() Method

This method will contain calls to methods that you have already used in this solution, so it should be easy to understand. However, it will also contain a call to the draw() method of the SBGSplash class. See Listing 2-22.

Listing 2-22. onDrawFrame

```
public void onDrawFrame(GL10 unused) {
GLES20.glClear(GLES20.GL_COLOR_BUFFER_BIT);
Matrix.setLookAtM(mVMatrix, 0, 0, 0, -3, 0f, 0f, 0f, 0f, 1.0f, 0.0f);
Matrix.multiplyMM(mMVPMatrix, 0, mProjMatrix, 0, mVMatrix, 0);
}
```

The final step in this solution is to set up the GLSurfaceView and call it from the main activity.

Create the GLSurfaceView

Create a new class called SBGGameView, as shown in Listing 2-23.

Listing 2-23. SBGGameView Class

```
importandroid.content.Context;
importandroid.opengl.GLSurfaceView;

public class SBGGameView extends GLSurfaceView {

public SBGGameView(Context context) {
super(context);

setRenderer(new SBGGameRenderer(context));

}
}
```

Notice that the only function of the GLSurfaceView is to set the Renderer to an instance of the Renderer that you created. Now you can set the GLSurfaceView as the main content view of your activity, as demonstrated in Listing 2-24.

Listing 2-24. Setting the GLSurfaceView

```
import com.jfdimarzio.superbanditguy.SBGGameView;
import android.os.Bundle;
import android.app.Activity;

public class MainActivity extends Activity {

private SBGGameViewgameView;

@Override
protected void onCreate(Bundle savedInstanceState) {
super.onCreate(savedInstanceState);
gameView = new SBGGameView(this);
setContentView(gameView);
}
}
```

You should now be able to compile and run your activity. The image should appear as shown in Figure 2-6.

Figure 2-6. Splash screen displayed using OpenGL ES

Now let's make sure the image shown using the emulator works the same way in the device.

Problem 2

OpenGL ES only displays a white image when using an Android device, but works fine when you are using the emulator.

Solution 2

Make sure the image resolution is a power of two.

How It Works

This is a fairly common problem, and luckily one that is easy to solve.

To avoid this *white box,* you must ensure that the resolutions of your images are a derivative of 2. The image for the splash (Figure 2-6) is 512 x 512. However I have found that 128 x 128 and 64 x 64 work as well.

Editing your images and resaving them in the proper resolution will fix this problem quickly.

2.3 Storing Images for Different Screen Resolutions

Problem

You have different images for different screen resolutions in your game.

Solution

Use the multiple `drawable-` folders in the `res` folder to store the correct resolution images.

How It Works

Android, as a platform, can support a myriad of different device screen resolutions. If you are creating different images for use on different devices screens, you will need to store those images in the correct place.

Table 2-1 offers some guidelines for where to store images, based on the intended device's screen resolution.

Table 2-1. Recommended Image Storage Locations

Folder	Resolution
res/drawable-ldpi	Up to 120 dpi
res/drawable-mdpi	From 120 to 160 dpi
res/drawable-hdpi	From 160 to 240 dpi
res/drawable-xhdpi	From 240 to 320 dpi
res/drawable-xxhdi	Over 320 dpi
res/drawable-nodpi	Any (non-specified) dpi

Chapter **3**

The Splash Screen

In this chapter, we are going to clear up some common problems that can occur when you are working on your game's splash screen. The splash screen, sometimes referred to as a title card, is the first thing the player sees when starting your game.

The splash screen can consist of one, or many, different images. These images are typically displayed when some background setup processes are running, and can represent anything from the development houses that worked on the game to the distribution company or agent.

Unless you are creating a game with no player setup required, you can use Android to load these splash screens in the main activity thread, before the game thread even begins. The reason for this is simple. Most games prompt the player with a menu screen before the game starts. The menu screen can have options for anything from starting the game, to review scores, to logging into a web-based service. If your game will include this kind of menu system, you will want to start the menu in the main activity thread. You can then let the menu spawn the game thread when the player chooses to start the game.

The solutions presented in this chapter assume that you will be launching the game's splash screen(s) in the main activity thread, not the game thread. Also, as covered in Chapter 2, this splash screen and menu screen examples will be in landscape mode. Why make a distinction about this? If you launch the splash screen in the main game thread, you could use OpenGL ES to display the screen, and then use your game code to track what the player is doing in the menu. While completely acceptable, this solution is a little overkill. It is much easier to code, and to keep track of, a solution where the splash screen is loaded and taken care of within the main activity thread.

3.1 Creating a Splash Screen
Problem

You are unable to display the name of the game while the game is loading in the background.

Solution

Use a splash screen to show information about the game while you perform other game-related functions in the background. The splash screen is generally an image that is displayed when your main Android activity is loaded. This means that you will load the image in the main activity thread, and start your game in a second thread.

How It Works

This solution is achieved in three easy steps. You will need to create a layout that displays the image you want to use as your splash screen. Then you will need to create a second `Activity` within your application that will represent your game. Finally, you will need to create a `postDelayed() Handler()` that will execute your background code and then start up your game thread when it is finished.

The end result is a game flow that follows this path: the main activity is started when the player launches your game, then a splash screen appears while your game does some housekeeping work in the background, and finally, when this housekeeping is complete, the activity launches directly into the game.

Create the Layout

First create a layout that displays your splash screen image. The instructions for creating this layout were explained in Chapter 2. The code for the `activity_main.xml` is shown in Listing 3-1. For a further explanation of what the code means, please see Chapter 2.

Listing 3-1. activity_main.xml

```
<RelativeLayoutxmlns:android="http://schemas.android.com/apk/res/android"
android:layout_width="match_parent"
android:layout_height="match_parent"
>

<ImageView
android:id="@+id/imageView1"
android:layout_width="match_parent"
android:layout_height="wrap_content"
android:layout_alignParentBottom="true"
android:contentDescription="@string/splash_screen_description"
android:layout_alignParentTop="true"
android:scaleType="fitXY"
android:src="@drawable/titlescreen" />

</RelativeLayout>
```

The image that is being displayed in the `activity_main.xml` file is show in Figure 3-1.

Figure 3-1. The game's splash screen

Create a New Activity

Now that your layout has been created, you need to create a new Activity within your application that will represent your game's main activity. The basic code for an Activity is shown in Listing 3-2.

Listing 3-2. The Basic Activity Code

```
public class SBGGame extends Activity{

@Override
public void onCreate(Bundle savedInstanceState) {
super.onCreate(savedInstanceState);

//Place your game code here

}
}
```

Right now you have the main Activity (with a layout that represents your splash screen), and you have the Activity that represents your game's main launching point. How to you get from the main Activity to the game Activity?

You are going to use a Handler() in the main Activity to delay the launch of the game Activity.

Create a postDelayed() Handler()

The Handler() has a method named postDelayed() that can be used to delay the start of another Activity intent. All of the housekeeping work that you need to perform can be done within the Handler(). Listings 3-3 through 3-6 will show you how.

In your main Activity, create a constant named GAME_THREAD_DELAYand set it to a value of 999000, as shown in Listing 3-3. This will represent a delay of 999 seconds before your game Activity is launched.

Listing 3-3. A Delayed Activity

```
public class MainActivity extends Activity {
static int GAME_THREAD_DELAY = 999000;

@Override
protected void onCreate(Bundle savedInstanceState) {
super.onCreate(savedInstanceState);

setContentView(R.layout.activity_main);
}

}
```

Now create a new instance of Handler(). Use the postDelayed() method to delay the launch of a new thread after the GAME_THREAD_DELAY has expired, as shown in Listing 3-4.

Listing 3-4. Using postDelayed

```
public class MainActivity extends Activity {
static int GAME_THREAD_DELAY = 999000;

@Override
protected void onCreate(Bundle savedInstanceState) {
super.onCreate(savedInstanceState);

setContentView(R.layout.activity_main);
new Handler().postDelayed(new Runnable() {
@Override
public void run() {
}
}, GAME_THREAD_DELAY);
}
}
```

Now place all of the housekeeping code, the code to launch the game Activity, and the code to kill the main Activity in the run() method of the new runnable object (see Listing 3-5).

Listing 3-5. Launching a New Activity

```
public class MainActivity extends Activity {
static int GAME_THREAD_DELAY = 999000;

@Override
protected void onCreate(Bundle savedInstanceState) {
super.onCreate(savedInstanceState);

setContentView(R.layout.activity_main);
new Handler().postDelayed(new Runnable() {
@Override
public void run() {

Intent gameMain = new Intent(MainActivity.this, SBGGame.class);
MainActivity.this.startActivity(gameMain);

//Perform all of your housekeeping activities here

MainActivity.this.finish();
}
}, GAME_THREAD_DELAY);
}

}
```

Finally, after all of the housekeeping activities are completed, change the GAME_THREAD_DELAY from 999 seconds to 1 second, forcing it to launch the game Activity, as shown in Listing 3-6. This gives you 999 seconds to perform all of your game's preloading. Then, when you are finished preloading the game, you simply set the delay to 1 second to force launch the game Activity.

Listing 3-6. Shortening the Delay Timer

```
public class MainActivity extends Activity {
static int GAME_THREAD_DELAY = 999000;

@Override
protected void onCreate(Bundle savedInstanceState) {
super.onCreate(savedInstanceState);

setContentView(R.layout.activity_main);
new Handler().postDelayed(new Thread() {
@Override
public void run() {
Intent gameMain = new Intent(MainActivity.this, SBGGame.class),
MainActivity.this.startActivity(gameMain);

//Perform all of your housekeeping activities here

GAME_THREAD_DELAY = 1000;

MainActivity.this.finish();
```

```
}
}, GAME_THREAD_DELAY);
}

}
```

3.2 Loading Multiple Images During a Splash Screen

Problem

You want to display multiple images in the splash screen while the game loads in the background.

Solution

Create a second layout, with a second splash screen image for the main `Activity`.

How It Works

This solution is going to build off of the solution to the last problem. In Problem 3.1, you created a `Handler()` in the main `Activity`. The `Handler()` performed some background tasks and then launched the game `Activity` when it was finished.

You are going to add a second layout to that solution that will be used to display a second image, or splash screen. The image that you will display in your second splash screen is shown in Figure 3-2.

Figure 3-2. The game's second splash screen

The first step is to create a new layout named second_image that will display the image. You can copy the xml from your first layout (Listing 3-1) to make things easy for yourself (presented here again for reference).

```xml
<RelativeLayout xmlns:android="http://schemas.android.com/apk/res/android"
android:layout_width="match_parent"
android:layout_height="match_parent"
>

<ImageView
android:id="@+id/imageView1"
android:layout_width="match_parent"
android:layout_height="wrap_content"
android:layout_alignParentBottom="true"
android:contentDescription="@string/splash_screen_two_description"
android:layout_alignParentTop="true"
android:scaleType="fitXY"
android:src="@drawable/credits" />

</RelativeLayout>
```

Now, modify your main Activity to show use this layout, as shown in Listing 3-7.

Listing 3-7. Loading a New Layout

```java
public class MainActivity extends Activity{

@Override
protected void onCreate(Bundle savedInstanceState) {
super.onCreate(savedInstanceState);

setContentView(R.layout.activity_main);
SBGVars.context = this;
new Handler().postDelayed(new Thread() {
@Override
public void run() {
setContentView(R.layout.second_image);
}
    }
}
```

When the Handler() delay expires, it will now display the second splash screen shown in Figure 3-2.

3.3 Fading In to and Out of a Splash Screen

Problem

The game's first splash screen should fade into the game's menu for a more subtle opening.

Solution

Use animation and the overridePendingTransition() to fade from one splash screen image to another.

How It Works

For this solution to work correctly, you need to start with the menu screen created in the Chapter 2.

What you want to do in this solution is create an animation that will fade from the main Activity's splash screen to the menu screen. This is not a hard task to accomplish; it requires the use of one method and a few layout files.

First, in the res/layout folder, create two new layout files; name one fadein.xml and the other fadeout.xml. The first will represent the layout for the animation that will fade an image into the display and the second will represent the layout for the animation that will fade an image out of the screen.

The code for the fadein.xml file should appear as shown in Listing 3-8.

Listing 3-8. fadein.xml

```
<?xml version="1.0" encoding="utf-8"?>
<alpha xmlns:android="http://schemas.android.com/apk/res/android"
android:interpolator="@android:anim/accelerate_interpolator"
android:fromAlpha="0.0"
android:toAlpha="1.0"
android:duration="1000" />
```

What this code says is that using the animation interpolator specified, move from a completely transparent (android:fromAlpha="0.0") to a completely opaque (android:toAlpha="1.0") state in one second (android:duration="1000").

In the fadeout.xml file, you are going to do roughly the same transition, only rather than going from transparent to opaque, you will go from opaque to transparent, as shown in Listing 3-9.

Listing 3-9. fadeout.xml

```
<?xml version="1.0" encoding="utf-8"?>
<alpha xmlns:android="http://schemas.android.com/apk/res/android"
android:interpolator="@android:anim/decelerate_interpolator"
android:fromAlpha="1.0"
android:toAlpha="0.0"
android:duration="1000" />
```

Now, within the Handler() that was explained in both Solutions 3.1 and 3.2, add a call to overridePendingTransition(), passing it a pointer to both the fadein.xml and fadeout.xml (see Listing 3-10).

Listing 3-10. Using overridePendingTransition()

```
public class MainActivity extends Activity
@Override
protected void onCreate(Bundle savedInstanceState) {
super.onCreate(savedInstanceState);

setContentView(R.layout.activity_main);
new Handler().postDelayed(new Thread() {
@Override
public void run() {
Intent mainMenu = new Intent(MainActivity.this, SBGMenuScreen.class);
MainActivity.this.startActivity(mainMenu);

//Perform background tasks

GAME_THREAD_DELAY = 1000;
MainActivity.this.finish();
overridePendingTransition(R.layout.fadein,R.layout.fadeout);
}
}, GAME_THREAD_DELAY);
}
}
```

When you start your game, you should now see the first splash screen load up, followed by a smooth second fade transition to the menu screen.

Chapter 4

The Menu Screen

You might have already built a game, or are in the process of building one, but still need a proper menu screen from which to launch it. Fear not. If you are having problems creating a working menu screen for your game, this chapter should be able to help you out.

In this chapter, you will find solutions for creating a two-button menu screen, wiring the buttons on said menu screen to start and exit the game, and many more problems that could arise while you create a menu.

The first solution will give you a proper, two-button menu screen for your game.

4.1 Create a Two-Button Menu Screen

Problem

Your game needs a menu screen for presenting options to the player.

Solution

Create a menu using an Android layout that has two buttons: one to start the game, and one to exit the game.

How It Works

While you don't have to use the full example, this solution works well with the splash screen created as a solution to the Chapter 3 problems. If you do want to use the solutions together, replace the creditscreen.xml from Chapter 3 (this is the layout that is faded into from the first splash screen) with the main_menu.xml that will be created in this solution.

The first step is to add some images to your project. The first image, shown in Figure 4-1, is the background for the menu screen. In this case, we are going to use the same image we used for the game splash screen, but feel free to use whatever image you want.

Figure 4-1. The menu screen background

Now you need two more images, one for each button. For this solution you are creating one button that will launch the game, and one button that will exit the game. Figures 4-2 and 4-3 represent the start button image and the exit button image, respectively.

Figure 4-2. The start button image

Figure 4-3. The exit button image

> **Note**   The images that I used in the finished solution consist of white text on a transparent background. However, for these images to be displayed properly in this book, the backgrounds were filled with grey.

Create a new xml layout named `main_menu.xml`. This layout will hold the new background image (in an `ImageView`) and the two buttons, using `ImageButton` nodes, as shown in Listing 4-1.

Listing 4-1. *main_menu.xml*

```xml
<?xml version="1.0" encoding="utf-8"?>
<RelativeLayout xmlns:android="http://schemas.android.com/apk/res/android"
xmlns:tools="http://schemas.android.com/tools"
android:layout_width="match_parent"
android:layout_height="match_parent"
tools:context=".SBGMenuScreen" >

<ImageView
android:id="@+id/imageView1"
android:layout_width="match_parent"
android:layout_height="wrap_content"
android:layout_alignParentBottom="true"
android:layout_alignParentTop="true"
android:contentDescription="@string/splash_screen_description"
android:scaleType="fitXY"
android:src="@drawable/titlescreen" />

<RelativeLayout
android:id="@+id/buttons"
android:layout_width="match_parent"
android:layout_height="wrap_content"
android:layout_alignParentBottom="true"
android:layout_marginBottom="20dp"
android:orientation="horizontal" >
</RelativeLayout>

<ImageButton
android:id="@+id/btnExit"
android:layout_width="wrap_content"
android:layout_height="wrap_content"
android:layout_above="@+id/buttons"
android:layout_alignParentRight="true"
android:layout_marginBottom="50dp"
android:layout_marginRight="55dp"
android:clickable="true"
android:contentDescription="@string/start_description"
android:src="@drawable/exit" />

<ImageButton
android:id="@+id/btnStart"
android:layout_width="wrap_content"
android:layout_height="wrap_content"
android:layout_alignParentLeft="true"
android:layout_alignTop="@+id/btnExit"
android:layout_marginLeft="48dp"
android:clickable="true"
android:contentDescription="@string/exit_description"
android:src="@drawable/start" />

</RelativeLayout>
```

Now that you have a layout for your menu, you need an `Activity` to display it. Create a new `Activity` in your game project; in this example, it will be named `SBGMenuScreen`. The `SBGMenuScreen` `Activity` should use `setContentView()` to display the new `main_menu` layout (see Listing 4-2).

Listing 4-2. SBGMenuScreen Layout

```
public class SBGMenuScreen extends Activity{

@Override
   public void onCreate(Bundle savedInstanceState) {
      super.onCreate(savedInstanceState);
      setContentView(R.layout.main_menu);
   }}
```

You now have a main menu that is displayed by an `Activity`, but where does it fit in with your game project?

You have two choices here. The first choice is to set `SBGMenuScreen` as the entry point for your game. The second is to use a splash screen to fade into the menu.

If you go with the first option, and set `SBGMenuScreen` as the main entry point for your game, then this will be the first screen seen by your player. In many cases, this could be a very valid solution and the example stops here for you. However, if you followed the solution in Chapter 3, and want to continue to use a splash screen, the rest of this solution will explain how to fit the menu in your splash screen.

Open the `MainActivity` from Chapter 3. This is where the splash screen is launched from. Change the references that have been bolded in Listing 4-3 to point to the new `SBGMenuScreenActivity` that you created.

Listing 4-3. Launching the Menu

```
public class MainActivity extends Activity {

@Override
protected void onCreate(Bundle savedInstanceState) {
super.onCreate(savedInstanceState);
int GAME_THREAD_DELAY = 4000;
setContentView(R.layout.activity_main);
new Handler().postDelayed(new Thread() {
@Override
public void run() {
Intent mainMenu = new Intent(MainActivity.this, SBGMenuScreen.class);
MainActivity.this.startActivity(mainMenu);
   MainActivity.this.finish();
overridePendingTransition(R.layout.fadein,R.layout.fadeout);
}
}, GAME_THREAD_DELAY);
}

}
```

No matter how you finished off your solution, the finished menu screen should appear as in Figure 4-4.

Figure 4-4. The menu screen

4.2 Wire Menu Buttons

Problem

The buttons do not respond when clicked.

Solution

Use OnClickListener() to react to button clicks.

How It Works

You have a menu for your game, like that in Solution 4.1. However, your buttons do not react when the player touches them. The solution for this is easier than you might think. All you have to do to fix this is create a couple of OnClickListener()s that will be used to listen for, and respond to, user interaction with your buttons.

This solution uses the Activity that is displaying your menu. If you created a menu using the solution in Recipe 4.1, then the file you need to open is the SBGMenuScreen. Listing 4-4 provides the current code for the menu Activity.

Listing 4-4. SBGMenuScreen

```
public class SBGMenuScreen extends Activity{

@Override
public void onCreate(Bundle savedInstanceState) {
super.onCreate(savedInstanceState);
setContentView(R.layout.main_menu);
}
```

The main_menu layout that is referred to in the SBGMenuScreen contains the following code. I am giving you the code to the main_menu layout because the solution is going to need to call elements from the layout. Therefore, you will have a reference to work from, just in case your menu layout does not match exactly.

```xml
<?xml version="1.0" encoding="utf-8"?>
<RelativeLayout xmlns:android="http://schemas.android.com/apk/res/android"
xmlns:tools="http://schemas.android.com/tools"
android:layout_width="match_parent"
android:layout_height="match_parent"
tools:context=".SBGMenuScreen" >

<ImageView
android:id="@+id/imageView1"
android:layout_width="match_parent"
android:layout_height="wrap_content"
android:layout_alignParentBottom="true"
android:layout_alignParentTop="true"
android:contentDescription="@string/splash_screen_description"
android:scaleType="fitXY"
android:src="@drawable/titlescreen" />

<RelativeLayout
android:id="@+id/buttons"
android:layout_width="match_parent"
android:layout_height="wrap_content"
android:layout_alignParentBottom="true"
android:layout_marginBottom="20dp"
android:orientation="horizontal" >
</RelativeLayout>

<ImageButton
android:id="@+id/btnExit"
android:layout_width="wrap_content"
android:layout_height="wrap_content"
android:layout_above="@+id/buttons"
android:layout_alignParentRight="true"
android:layout_marginBottom="50dp"
android:layout_marginRight="55dp"
android:clickable="true"
android:contentDescription="@string/start_description"
android:src="@drawable/exit" />

<ImageButton
android:id="@+id/btnStart"
android:layout_width="wrap_content"
android:layout_height="wrap_content"
android:layout_alignParentLeft="true"
android:layout_alignTop="@+id/btnExit"
android:layout_marginLeft="48dp"
android:clickable="true"
```

```
android:contentDescription="@string/exit_description"
android:src="@drawable/start" />

</RelativeLayout>
```

The first step in the solution is to create a pair of ImageButton variables and set them to the image buttons used in your menu layout. The method that you will use to set your variables to your image buttons is findViewById().

> **Tip**   Because findViewById() does not inherently know the type of the view you are finding, be sure to case the result as the proper type before assigning it.

Listing 4-5. findViewByIf

```
public class SBGMenuScreen extends Activity{

@Override
    public void onCreate(Bundle savedInstanceState) {
        super.onCreate(savedInstanceState);
        setContentView(R.layout.main_menu);
ImageButton start = (ImageButton)findViewById(R.id.btnStart);
        ImageButton exit = (ImageButton)findViewById(R.id.btnExit);

    }
}
```

All views have the method setOnClickListener(). You will use this method to assign a new OnClickListener() to the specific button.That is all you need to complete the solution.

Listing 4-6. setOnClickListener

```
public class SBGMenuScreen extends Activity{

@Override
public void onCreate(Bundle savedInstanceState) {
super.onCreate(savedInstanceState);
setContentView(R.layout.main_menu);

ImageButton start = (ImageButton)findViewById(R.id.btnStart);
ImageButton exit = (ImageButton)findViewById(R.id.btnExit);

start.setOnClickListener(new OnClickListener(){
@Override
public void onClick(View v) {

//TODO all of your startup code

}

});
```

```
exit.setOnClickListener(new OnClickListener(){
@Override
public void onClick(View v) {

//TODO all of your exit code

}
});

    }
}
```

Each OnClickListener() has an OnClick() method. The code within the OnClick() method will be executed each time the OnClickListener() for that button is tripped. Replace the TODO comments with the code that you wish to execute when the player presses the start or exit buttons, respectively.

4.3 Launch a Game Thread

Problem

The game thread needs to start when the player presses the Start Game button on the menu.

Solution

Launch the game Activity from within the OnClick() method of the start button.

How It Works

This is a relatively simple solution that will have you adding a couple of lines of code to your OnClick() method for the start button. If you already have an Activity that is used to start your game, use that here. If you do not yet have an Activity for your game, create a basic Activity, as shown in Listing 4-7.

Listing 4-7. A Basic Activity

```
public class SBGGameMain extends Activity {

private SBGGameView gameView;

@Override
public void onCreate(Bundle savedInstanceState) {
super.onCreate(savedInstanceState);
//The content view here represents the GLSurfaceView
//for your game
gameView = new SBGGameView(this);
setContentView(gameView);
}
```

```
@Override
protected void onResume() {
super.onResume();
gameView.onResume();
}

@Override
protected void onPause() {
super.onPause();
gameView.onPause();
}

}
```

Again, if you already have an Activity created for your game, use that in place of this in your solution.

The only step you need to take to launch your game is to modify the OnClick() method of the OnClickListener() attached to your start button. Simply create a new Intent for the game Activty and start it from inside the OnClick(), as shown in Listing 4-8.

Listing 4-8. Launching an Activity from onClick()

```
start.setOnClickListener(new OnClickListener(){
@Override
public void onClick(View v) {
//Start the game
Intent game = new Intent(getApplicationContext(),SBGGameMain.class);
SBGMenuScreen.this.startActivity(game);

}

});
```

Now when the player presses the start button, your menu will launch cleanly into the game.

4.4 Exit a Game Thread Cleanly

Problem

The game needs to clean up any threads and running processes when it is exited.

Solution

Create a method that closes open items before the game is exited. Then, kill the game thread.

How It Works

This is a two-part solution that involves creating a single method that can be called to complete any housekeeping before the game exits, and then kills the game thread.

Before your player closes your game, you might want to take care of tasks such as saving player data, updating statistics to a central server, or even killing any background music that is playing. To do this, you will need to create a method somewhere in your game that can be called from the main menu.

In Listing 4-9, I have created a method called onExit(). Within onExit(), I am killing some background music that is playing in my game. Again, you add whatever code you need to perform your housekeeping to onExit(). The important part of the method is that is returns a Boolean. A result of true means that everything has been taken care of and the game is good to exit, while a result of false will need to be handled further before the game can exit.

Listing 4-9. onExit()

```
public boolean onExit(View v) {
try
{
//Sample code to stop some background music
Intent bgmusic = new Intent(context, SFMusic.class);
context.stopService(bgmusic);
musicThread.stop();

return true;
}catch(Exception e){
return false;

}

}
```

> **Tip** The onExit() method can be anywhere in your project as long as it has visibility to everything that you want do within it.

Now, modify your OnClick() method for you exit button's OnClickListener() to call onExit() (see Listing 4-10).

Listing 4-10. Calling onExit()

```
exit.setOnClickListener(new OnClickListener(){
@Override
public void onClick(View v) {
boolean clean = false;
clean = onExit(v);
if (clean)
{
}
}
});
```

Finally, assuming that your onExit() returned a true result, kill the current process and exit (see Listing 4-11).

Listing 4-11. Killing the Game Process

```
exit.setOnClickListener(new OnClickListener(){
@Override
public void onClick(View v) {
boolean clean = false;
clean = engine.onExit(v);
if (clean)
{
int pid= android.os.Process.myPid();
android.os.Process.killProcess(pid);
}
}
});
```

4.5 Swap Menu Button Images

Problem

Menu buttons should change color or image when clicked.

Solution

Point the source of the button's image to an xml selector that controls the swapping on images.

How It Works

You might want your game's menu to have an added punch to it by changing the menu's button images when the player selects them. You can easily achieve this by creating an xml selector that holds pointers to the images you want, and the states under which to display them. Then, in your layout file, replace the source pointer to the button's original image file with that of your xml selector.

For this solution, you will be swapping between the images in Figures 4-2 and 4-3 with those in Figures 4-5 and 4-6 when the player selects the appropriate button.

Figure 4-5. The new start button image

Figure 4-6. The new exit button image

The original button images are referred to as @drawable/start and @drawable/exit, respectively. The new files, once added to the drawable folder, will be @drawable/newstart and @drawable/newexit. You can accomplish this in three steps.

The first step is to create a new xml file named startselector.xml and be sure to place it in the drawable folder with the images. This is not the usual place for xml files. Normally, you would think of putting an xml file into the layout folder. However, because this file is going to be substituted for an image source, it needs to be placed in the drawable folder.

Open the startselector.xmlfile and create the xml selector shown in Listing 4-12.

Listing 4-12. startselector.xml

```
<?xml version="1.0" encoding="utf-8"?>
<selector
xmlns:android="http://schemas.android.com/apk/res/android">
<item android:drawable="@drawable/start" />
<item android:state_pressed="true" android:drawable="@drawable/newstart"  />
</selector>
```

The two items in the selector indicate the different states for which you want to swap out the image. The first item is the default state. This is the image that will be displayed under idle conditions. The second item is only displayed when the state_pressed is true. Therefore, when the button is pressed, the selector will send it the newstart image to be displayed.

Create a second selector xml file named exitselector.xml, as shown in Listing 4-13. The file should be formatted the same as the startselector.xml file, though it will be used to change the exit button images.

Listing 4-13. exitselector.xml

```
<?xml version="1.0" encoding="utf-8"?>
<selector
xmlns:android="http://schemas.android.com/apk/res/android">
<item android:drawable="@drawable/exit" />
<item android:state_pressed="true" android:drawable="@drawable/newexit"  />
</selector>
```

The last step to this solution is to change the layout file for your menu. Change the image source for each button to point to the appropriate selector rather than the image file (see Listing 4-14).

Listing 4-14. main_menu.xml

```
<?xml version="1.0" encoding="utf-8"?>
<RelativeLayout xmlns:android="http://schemas.android.com/apk/res/android"
xmlns:tools="http://schemas.android.com/tools"
android:layout_width="match_parent"
android:layout_height="match_parent"
tools:context=".SBGMenuScreen" >
```

```
<ImageView
android:id="@+id/imageView1"
android:layout_width="match_parent"
android:layout_height="wrap_content"
android:layout_alignParentBottom="true"
android:layout_alignParentTop="true"
android:contentDescription="@string/splash_screen_description"
android:scaleType="fitXY"
android:src="@drawable/titlescreen" />

<RelativeLayout
android:id="@+id/buttons"
android:layout_width="match_parent"
android:layout_height="wrap_content"
android:layout_alignParentBottom="true"
android:layout_marginBottom="20dp"
android:orientation="horizontal" >
</RelativeLayout>

<ImageButton
android:id="@+id/btnExit"
android:layout_width="wrap_content"
android:layout_height="wrap_content"
android:layout_above="@+id/buttons"
android:layout_alignParentRight="true"
android:layout_marginBottom="50dp"
android:layout_marginRight="55dp"
android:clickable="true"
android:contentDescription="@string/start_description"
android:src="@drawable/exitselector" />

<ImageButton
android:id="@+id/btnStart"
android:layout_width="wrap_content"
android:layout_height="wrap_content"
android:layout_alignParentLeft="true"
android:layout_alignTop="@+id/btnExit"
android:layout_marginLeft="48dp"
android:clickable="true"
android:contentDescription="@string/exit_description"
android:src="@drawable/startselector" />

</RelativeLayout>
```

4.6 Lock the Screen Orientation

Problem

The menu screen should not change orientation when the device is moved between landscape and portrait mode.

Solution

Lock the screen orientation so that it cannot change.

How It Works

This is a rather easy solution to a common problem. The quickest way to achieve this is to manually edit the project's `AndroidManifest.xml` file. The manifest file contains the project's main settings for its activities. It is a good idea to lock all of the screens for your game on specific orientation.

Locate the activity tag for your main menu's `Activity` and lock it to landscape mode, as shown here:

```
<activity android:name="SBGMenuScreen" android:screenOrientation="landscape"></activity>
```

Reading Player Input

Chapter 5

If this is your first time coding a game for a mobile device or tablet, you are likely to quickly notice that there is a distinct lack of input options to relay your player's intentions back into the game code. Without the benefit of game controllers, keyboards, or mice, it can be very hard to supply your player with a complex input system.

Wiring up your game to detect and respond to touch events on the device is not as hard as it might appear on the surface.

Let's take a look at some of the more common problems in using a touch screen as a game input.

5.1 Detect a Screen Touch

Problem

Your game is unable to detect when the player has touched the screen.

Solution

Use the onTouchEvent() to detect where and when the player touches the screen.

How It Works

Your Android game is launched from a class that extends Activity. This class will be used to detect and react to touch events that happen in your game. Keep in mind the code for your game, and the game loop, will be running in a GLSurfaceView via a Renderer. However, you will still be using the Activity that launched your game to track the input from the player on the screen.

Within your `Activity`, override the `onTouchEvent()` as follows:

```
@Override
public boolean onTouchEvent(MotionEvent event) {
}
```

The `onTouchEvent()` takes in a `MotionEvent`. This `MotionEvent` is automatically passed in by the system when the event call is generated.

The `MotionEvent` contains all of the information that you would need to help determine and decipher the action of the player. From the `MotionEvent`, you get information such as the x and y coordinates where the player touched, the pressure and duration of the touch, and you can even determine the direction of a swipe movement.

For example, here you are simply getting the player's touch coordinates:

```
@Override
public boolean onTouchEvent(MotionEvent event) {
float x = event.getX();
float y = event.getY();
}
```

You can now react to the x and y coordinates, as you see fit.

5.2 Detect a Screen Multi-touch

Problem

Your game is unable to detect multiple screen touches at the same time with `onTouchEvent()`.

Solution

Use `getPointerCount()` and `PointerCoords` to help retrieve the pointer objects for detecting multi-touch input.

How It Works

The `MotionEvent` that is passed into `onTouchEvent()` can track up to five distinct simultaneous screen touches. The concept here is to loop through all of the pointers that were detected using `getPointerCount()`. Inside of the loop, you are

going to use `getPointerID()` to retrieve the information that you need for each pointer.

Begin by setting up your `onTouchEvent()` and looping through the detected pointers, as shown in Listing 5-1.

Listing 5-1. onTouchEvent()

```
@Override
public boolean onTouchEvent(MotionEvent event) {

MotionEvent.PointerCoords[] coords = new MotionEvent.PointerCoords[event.getPointerCount()];

    For(int i = 0; i< event.getPointerCount(); i++)
    {
event.getPointerCoords(i, coords[i]);
    }
}
```

You can now get all of the information that you need, from each pointer that was detected. Pass the coord[] into your game loop and you will have access to the x and y coordinates of each touch point. You will also have the touch point's orientation, pressure, size (area), and the length of major and minor axes.

5.3 Divide the Screen into Touch Zones

Problem

You need to determine whether the player touched the right or left side of the screen.

Solution

Use the height and width of the screen to determine which side of the screen the player touched.

How It Works

You know how to use the onTouchEvent() to determine if and when the player has touched the screen, and the coordinates that the play touched. This is very useful information when you are trying to create an input system for your game. The problem you now face is in trying to establish whether the x and y coordinates that you have been given fall within a specific area of the screen.

Let's say you are creating a platform game where the player can run to the left and to the right. You have set up your onTouchEvent() and you are trapping the x and y coordinates each time the player touches the screen. How can you easily determine whether those coordinates should push the player to the left or to the right?

The answer is to divide the screen into touch zones. In this case, we would want one zone on the left-hand side of the screen, and one zone on the right-hand side of the screen. A few simple if statements can then be used to check the locations on the screen that the player touched.

Using the example of a platform game, where the only directions the player can move are to the left and to the right, you can divide the screen into two halves—one representing the left and one the right. You might also want to consider placing the touch zones toward the bottom of the screen, where a player's thumbs are likely to be.

This means that you would have to ignore any touch coordinates that fall above the left and right touch zones. Take a look at Figures 5-1 and 5-2 for a visual representation of this concept.

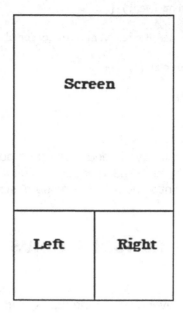

Figure 5-1. *Portrait mode with left and right touch zones*

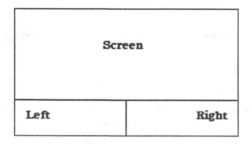

Figure 5-2. *Landscape mode with left and right touch zones*

The first step to create touch zones is to get the height of the screen. To do this, create a new `Display` property on a common class, as follows:

```
public static Display display;
```

On the main `Activity` for your application, use the `WINDOW_SERVICE` to copy the default display to this property, as shown in Listing 5-2.

Listing 5-2. *Using* `WINDOW_SERVICE`

```
MyClass.display = ((WindowManager) getSystemService(Context.WINDOW_SERVICE)).getDefaultDisplay();
```

You can now determine the height and width of the screen from within your game code, as shown in Listing 5-3.

Listing 5-3. determine the height and width

```
@Override
public boolean onTouchEvent(MotionEvent event) {
//Get the non-touchable area of the screen -
//the upper two-thirds of the screen
int height = MyClass.display.getHeight() / 3;

//The playable area is now the lower third of the screen
int playableArea = MyClass.display.getHeight() - height;
}
```

> **Caution** This method works, but is only fully effective if your game uses the full screen as this one does. If your game is not going to use the full screen, wait until after the game's view loads and call `<view>.getHeight()`.

Using the value `playableArea` as a y-axis value, you can easily tell whether your player is touching the correct part of the screen. Create a simple `if` statement to test the locations of the player's touch coordinates (see Listing 5-4).

Listing 5-4. Using playableArea

```
@Override
public boolean onTouchEvent(MotionEvent event) {
//Get the non-touchable area of the screen -
//the upper two-thirds of the screen
int height = MyClass.display.getHeight() / 3;

//The playable area is now the lower third of the screen
 int playableArea = MyClass.display.getHeight() - height;

if (y > playableArea){

//This y coordinate is within the touch zone

}
}
```

Now that you know the player has touched the correct area of the screen, the left and right and sides of the touch zone can be determined by testing whether the x coordinate is greater than or less than the center point of the screen (see Listing 5-5) .

Listing 5-5. Testing the Touch Zones

```
@Override
public boolean onTouchEvent(MotionEvent event) {
//Get the non-touchable area of the screen -
//the upper two-thirds of the screen
int height = MyClass.display.getHeight() / 3;

//Get the center point of the screen
int center = MyClass.display.getWidth() / 2;

//The playable area is now the lower third of the screen
int playableArea = MyClass.display.getHeight() - height;

if (y > playableArea){

//This y coordinate is within the touch zone

if(x < center){
//The player touched the left
}else{
//The player touched the right
}

}
}
```

You have successfully determined whether the player has touched the left- or right-hand side of the screen. Replace the comments with your specific code to initiate actions based on where the player touched.

5.4 Detect a Screen Swipe

Problem

You need to determine whether the player swiped or flinged the screen and in what direction.

Solution

Use SimpleOnGestureListener and then calculate the direction of a fling.

How It Works

For some games—think Temple Run—you want to let the user swipe or fling the screen to indicate which direction they want to move. A fling upward could represent a jump, for example. This could be a much more versatile method of player input, but it also requires a slight bit more setup code.

The code needed to implement this will go on the same Activity as the OnTouchEvent(). In fact, you can use the two—OnTouchEvent() and SimpleOnGestureListener—in conjunction with each other.

Open your `Activity` and instantiate a `SimpleInGestureListener`, as follows:

```
GestureDetector.SimpleOnGestureListener gestureListener = new GestureDetector.
SimpleOnGestureListener(){
};
```

There are several methods that you need to implement within the gesture listener. However, the only one you will be working with in this solution is `OnFling()`, which is provided in Listing 5-6.

Listing 5-6. OnFling()

```
GestureDetector.SimpleOnGestureListener gestureListener = new GestureDetector.
SimpleOnGestureListener(){
@Override
public boolean onDown(MotionEvent arg0) {
//TODO Auto-generated method stub
return false;
}

@Override
public boolean onFling(MotionEvent e1, MotionEvent e2, float velocityX,
float velocityY) {
//React to the fling action
return false;
}
@Override
public void onLongPress(MotionEvent e) {
//TODO Auto-generated method stub

}
@Override
public boolean onScroll(MotionEvent e1, MotionEvent e2, float distanceX,
float distanceY) {
//TODO Auto-generated method stub
return false;
}
@Override
public void onShowPress(MotionEvent e) {
//TODO Auto-generated method stub

}
@Override
public boolean onSingleTapUp(MotionEvent e) {
//TODO Auto-generated method stub
return false;
}

};
```

Now, create a new variable in your `Activity`, as follows:

```
private GestureDetector gd;
```

The GestureDetector will be used to throw the gesture event. Initialize the detector in the onCreate() of the Activity, as follows:

```
@Override
public void onCreate(Bundle savedInstanceState) {
super.onCreate(savedInstanceState);
gd = new GestureDetector(this,gestureListener);
}
```

Finally, in the OnTouchEvent(), throw to the gestureListener, like so:

```
@Override
public boolean onTouchEvent(MotionEvent event) {
return gd.onTouchEvent(event);
}
```

When the player flings the screen, the code in the OnFling()method will be executed. This takes care of the what and when;next you need to determine what direction.

Notice that OnFling() takes two MotionEvent attributes. Since you have used it earlier, you know that the MotionEvent contains a getX() and a getY() for getting you the respective coordinates of the event.

The two events (e1 and e2) represent the start point and end point of the fling. Therefore, using the x and y coordinates of each event, you can calculate which direction the player moved (see Listing 5-7).

Listing 5-7. Detecting Fling Motion

```
float leftMotion = e1.getX() - e2.getX();
float upMotion = e1.getY() - e2.getY();

float rightMotion = e2.getX() - e1.getX();
float downMotion = e2.getY() - e1.getY();

if((leftMotion == Math.max(leftMotion, rightMotion)) && (leftMotion > Math.max(downMotion,
upMotion)) )
{
//The player moved left
}

if((rightMotion == Math.max(leftMotion, rightMotion)) && rightMotion > Math.max(downMotion, upMotion) )
{
//The player moved right
}
if((upMotion == Math.max(upMotion, downMotion)) && (upMotion > Math.max(leftMotion, rightMotion)) )
{
//The player moved up
}

if((downMotion == Math.max(upMotion, downMotion)) && (downMotion > Math.max(leftMotion, rightMotion)) )
{
//The player moved down
}
```

Now you can fill in the appropriate code for the action you need to take in your game.

Because this solution jumped around the Activity a bit, Listing 5-8 shows what the finished Activity should look like.

Listing 5-8. Full Code for SBGGameMain

```
public class SBGGameMain extends Activity {
private GestureDetector gd;

@Override
public void onCreate(Bundle savedInstanceState) {
super.onCreate(savedInstanceState);
setContentView(myContentView);
gd = new GestureDetector(this,gestureListener);
}
@Override
protected void onResume() {
super.onResume();
}

@Override
protected void onPause() {
super.onPause();
}

@Override
public boolean onTouchEvent(MotionEvent event) {
return gd.onTouchEvent(event);
}

GestureDetector.SimpleOnGestureListener gestureListener = new GestureDetector.
SimpleOnGestureListener(){
@Override
public boolean onDown(MotionEvent arg0) {
//TODO Auto-generated method stub
return false;
}

@Override
public boolean onFling(MotionEvent e1, MotionEvent e2, float velocityX,
float velocityY) {

float leftMotion = e1.getX() - e2.getX();
float upMotion = e1.getY() - e2.getY();

float rightMotion = e2.getX() - e1.getX();
float downMotion = e2.getY() - e1.getY();
```

```
if((leftMotion == Math.max(leftMotion, rightMotion)) && (leftMotion > Math.max(downMotion, upMotion)) )
{

}

if((rightMotion == Math.max(leftMotion, rightMotion)) && rightMotion > Math.max(downMotion, upMotion) )
{

}
if((upMotion == Math.max(upMotion, downMotion)) && (upMotion > Math.max(leftMotion, rightMotion)) )
{

}

if((downMotion == Math.max(upMotion, downMotion)) && (downMotion > Math.max(leftMotion, rightMotion)) )
{

}
return false;
}
@Override
public void onLongPress(MotionEvent e) {
//TODO Auto-generated method stub

}
@Override
public boolean onScroll(MotionEvent e1, MotionEvent e2, float distanceX,
float distanceY) {
//TODO Auto-generated method stub
return false;
}
@Override
public void onShowPress(MotionEvent e) {
//TODO Auto-generated method stub

}
@Override
public boolean onSingleTapUp(MotionEvent e) {
//TODO Auto-generated method stub
return false;
}

};
}
```

5.5 Use the Device Accelerometer

Problem

The game character does not move when the player tilts the device.

Solution

Use the device's built-in accelerometer to detect when the device has been tilted in a specific direction, and then move the character accordingly.

How It Works

Most, if not all, Android devices include an accelerometer. One popular use for this sensor is as another input device for a game. Using feedback from the accelerometer, you can detect whether the player has tilted the device and then react accordingly in the code.

In Listing 5-9, you detect whether the player has tilted the phone left or right, and then set the proper variables to move the character in the tilted direction. First, implement SensorEventListener in your Activity class. Then allow Eclipse (or your IDE of choice) add in the required method overrides.

Listing 5-9. SensorEvenListener

```
public class SBGGameMain extends Activity implements SensorEventListener{
@Override
public void onCreate(Bundle savedInstanceState) {
//TODO Auto-generated method stub
}
@Override
protected void onResume() {
//TODO Auto-generated method stub
}
@Override
protected void onPause() {
//TODO Auto-generated method stub
}
@Override
public void onAccuracyChanged(Sensor sensor, int accuracy) {
//TODO Auto-generated method stub

}
@Override
public void onSensorChanged(SensorEvent event) {
//TODO Auto-generated method stub
}

}
```

Several variables are needed. prevX and prevY track the previous x and y axis tilt location to determine whether there has been a change in tilting. A Boolean, isInitialized, determines whether a tilt has been previously detected; if not, new values are stored in prevX and prevY. A static float, NOISE, holds a value that lets you determine a real tilt change, from ambient device movement. Finally, variables for the SensorManager and accelerometer are set up. See Listing 5-10.

Listing 5-10. SensorManager

```
public class SBGGameMain extends Activity implements SensorEventListener{
private float prevX;
private float prevY;
private boolean isInitialized;
private final float NOISE = (float) 2.0;
private SensorManager sensorManager;
private Sensor accelerometer;
@Override
public void onCreate(Bundle savedInstanceState) {
//TODO Auto-generated method stub
}
@Override
protected void onResume() {
//TODO Auto-generated method stub
}
@Override
protected void onPause() {
//TODO Auto-generated method stub
}
@Override
public void onAccuracyChanged(Sensor sensor, int accuracy) {
//TODO Auto-generated method stub

}
@Override
public void onSensorChanged(SensorEvent event) {
//TODO Auto-generated method stub
}

}
```

Next, perform some housekeeping in the onCreate(), onPause(), and onResume()methods before performing the core of the code in the onSensorChanged() method (see Listing 5-11).

Listing 5-11. onSensorChanged

```
@Override
public void onCreate(Bundle savedInstanceState) {
super.onCreate(savedInstanceState);
gameView = new SBGGameView(this);
setContentView(gameView);

isInitialized= false;
sensorManager= (SensorManager) getSystemService(this.SENSOR_SERVICE);
accelerometer= sensorManager.getDefaultSensor(Sensor.TYPE_ACCELEROMETER);
sensorManager.registerListener(this, accelerometer, SensorManager.SENSOR_DELAY_NORMAL);

}
```

```
Override
protected void onResume() {
super.onResume();

sensorManager.registerListener(this, accelerometer, SensorManager.SENSOR_DELAY_NORMAL);

gameView.onResume();

}

@Override
protected void onPause() {
super.onPause();

sensorManager.unregisterListener(this);

gameView.onPause();
}
```

Now for the core of the solution. The onSensorChanged()method is fired when a change in the sensor is detected; in this case, that is the accelerometer. Trap the change, and use the x and y vectors to set your PLAYER_MOVE_LEFT and PLAYER_MOVE_JUMP, as shown in Listing 5-12.

Listing 5-12. setting the player action

```
public class SBGGameMain extends Activity implements SensorEventListener{
private float prevX;
private float prevY;
private boolean isInitialized;
private final float NOISE = (float) 2.0;
private SensorManager sensorManager;
private Sensor accelerometer;

@Override
public void onCreate(Bundle savedInstanceState) {
super.onCreate(savedInstanceState);
gameView = new SBGGameView(this);
setContentView(gameView);

isInitialized= false;
sensorManager= (SensorManager) getSystemService(this.SENSOR_SERVICE);
accelerometer= sensorManager.getDefaultSensor(Sensor.TYPE_ACCELEROMETER);
sensorManager.registerListener(this, accelerometer, SensorManager.SENSOR_DELAY_NORMAL);

}
@Override
protected void onResume() {
super.onResume();
```

```
sensorManager.registerListener(this, accelerometer, SensorManager.SENSOR_DELAY_NORMAL);

gameView.onResume();

}

@Override
protected void onPause() {
super.onPause();

sensorManager.unregisterListener(this);

gameView.onPause();
}

@Override
public void onAccuracyChanged(Sensor sensor, int accuracy) {
//TODO Auto-generated method stub

}
@Override
public void onSensorChanged(SensorEvent event) {
float x = event.values[0];
float y = event.values[1];
if (!isInitialized) {
prevX = x;
prevY = y;
isInitialized = true;
} else {
float deltaX = Math.abs(prevX - x);
float deltaY = Math.abs(prevY - y);
if (deltaX < NOISE) deltaX = (float)0.0;
if (deltaY < NOISE) deltaY = (float)0.0;
prevX = x;
prevY = y;
if (deltaX > deltaY) {
playeraction = PLAYER_MOVE_LEFT;
} else if (deltaY > deltaX) {
playeraction = PLAYER_MOVE_JUMP;
} else {

}
}
}
}
```

Chapter 6

Loading a SpriteSheet

Chances are that by this point, you have the shell or beginnings of a game on the Android platform. It is also possible that you have tried to animate one or all of your characters, weapons, or other on-screen object without luck.

If you have tried to load separate images, you no doubt found the process of flipping those images to create animation painfully slow. The solution to this problem is almost as old as video games themselves:sprite sheets. Most 2D-based video games still employ an animation technique that is well-tested, and well-suited for the task; that is, creating a sprite sheet of the animation frames needed in your game.

In this chapter, you will walk through some solutions to common problems using sprite sheets.

6.1 Use a Sprite Sheet

Problem

Loading multiple, separate images for animation takes up too much space and is slow.

Solution

Use a sprite sheet that contains all of your animation frames in one image file.

How It Works

Let's start with the basics. A sprite sheet is a single image file that holds all of the different images that can be used to create an animated sprite.

The main character for our sample game—Super Bandit Guy—should be able to run left and right across the screen. This requires that the sprite for Super Bandit Guy be animated when he runs. Rather than create a separate image for each frame of the animation (which would be so resource intensive that the final game might not even load), each image in the animation is loaded into a single file called a sprite sheet. Figure 6-1 shows a detail of the sprite sheet for Super Bandit Guy's running animation.

Figure 6-1. Super Bandit Guy running (detail)

Notice that the different frames of animation are all placed in a single file, thus reducing the resources needed to store, recall, swap, and display separate images.

Drop the image into your res/drawable folder. This is the same process used for any other image file. All image files can be stored in the res/drawable folders and then easily recalled by id using R.drawable.<imagename>. However, remember that all image names must be lowercase or you will not be able to call them back.

The question now is this: how do you display only one frame at a time instead of the entire sprite sheet at once? This is actually easier than it seems. Using OpenGL ES, you are going to size this image, or texture, so that the one frame of animation you want show will fit on the vertices at a time (explained in the next solution). Keep in mind, in OpenGL ES your textures and your vertices can be different sizes.

> **Note** Just because all of the images used by OpenGL ES must be square, does not mean that every space in the sprite sheet must contain a frame of animation. While the 4x4sheet we are using for Super Bandit Guy can hold 16 frames of animation, we are only using 10.

Figure 6-2 shows the sprite sheet that is being used for Super Bandit Guy.

Figure 6-2. Super Bandit Guy (full sprite sheet)

Note   The backgrounds of the images have been tinted grey for the purposes of showing them in this book. Ideally, your images should have transparent backgrounds.

6.2 Access Images in the Sprite Sheet
Problem
Displaying a sprite sheet shows the entire image, instead of the individual image that is needed.

Solution
Adjust the texture mapping to display the portion of the sprite sheet that is needed.

How It Works
To understand how this solution works, you need to first understand that the vertices which your texture is mapped to, and the texture object itself, are treated are two separate entities that can be manipulated independently of each other. What this means is that you can resize, move, or alter the texture without affecting the vertices.

You already know that the sprite sheet in Figure 6-2 contains all of the frames of animation needed to make Super Bandit Guy appear as though he is running. However, if you tried to use the sprite sheet as a texture, two things would become immediately apparent. First, the texture appears upside down; and second, the entire sprite sheet is mapped onto the vertices, rather than just one frame of animation.

When OpenGL creates a texture, an image is loaded into a byte array. When the image is loaded into the array, the first byte of the image is loaded into the back of the array, followed by the second byte, and so on. As OpenGL starts to read the texture information from the array, the first byte it reads (the first byte in the array) is actually the last byte that came out of the file. Therefore, OpenGL's texture is a reversed version of your original image.

You need to flip the texture within OpenGL to make it appear right-sideup. Then you need to adjust the size of the texture that is mapped to your vertices so that only one frame of the sprite sheet is visible. Figure 6-3 illustrates this concept.

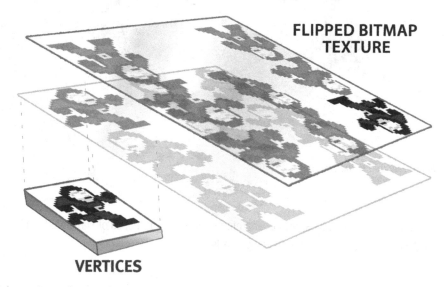

FLIPPED BITMAP TEXTURE

VERTICES

Figure 6-3. Flipping and mapping a sprite sheet texture onto a vertex

First, let's take care of flipping the image so that it appears right-side up.

> **Tip**   OpenGL ES handles the loading of all images into textures the same way, regardless of whether they are sprite sheets. Therefore, all of your images will always appear reversed when they become textures. This step of the solution should be performed when loading all of your textures.

In the code that you have written to load your images into textures, instantiate a new Matrix and use the postScale() method to create new matrix that flips the texture along the y axis. The new matrix is passed into the createBitmap() method that is normally used to load textures.

In Listing 6-1, texture represents the reference id of the image you want to load, which is found in the drawable folder.

Listing 6-1. Using postScale()

```
InputStreamimagestream = context.getResources().openRawResource(texture);
Bitmap bitmap = null;
Bitmap temp = null;

Matrix mtrx = new Matrix();
mtrx.postScale(1f, -1f);

temp = BitmapFactory.decodeStream(imagestream);
bitmap = Bitmap.createBitmap(temp, 0, 0, temp.getWidth(), temp.getHeight(), mtrx, true);

imagestream.close();
imagestream = null;
```

Now that your texture is flipped the correct way, it is time to adjust the texture so that only one frame is visibly mapped to your vertices. Again, this can be done on load, when the textures and vertices are built.

The code that you currently have for loading your textures, in part, should look like Listing 6-2.

Listing 6-2. Texture Array

```
privateFloatBuffervertexBuffer;
privateFloatBuffertextureBuffer;
privateByteBufferindexBuffer;

private float[] vertices = {
0f, 0f, 0f,
1f, 0f, 0f,
1f, 1f, 0f,
0f, 1f, 0f,
};

private float[] texture = {
0f, 0f,
1f, 0f,
1f, 1f,
0f, 1f,
};
```

Because the default coordinate system in OpenGL ES goes from 0 to 1, the texture array in Listing 6-2 uses the entire texture. The full texture will be mapped onto the vertices using this array. However, given the sprite sheet in Figure 6-2, you only want to see one-quarter of the sprite sheet at a time

> **Note**   The sprite sheet in Figure 6-2 is divided into four rows of four images (not all are used). Therefore, each row is 25 percent of the height of the overall texture, and each column is 25 percent of the width of the overall texture.

Correct the texture array, as shown in Listing 6-3, to display only one frame of animation from your sprite sheet.

Listing 6-3. New Texture Array

```
privateFloatBuffervertexBuffer;
privateFloatBuffertextureBuffer;
privateByteBufferindexBuffer;

private float[] vertices = {
0f, 0f, 0f,
1f, 0f, 0f,
1f, 1f, 0f,
0f, 1f, 0f,
};

private float[] texture = {
0f, 0f,
.25f, 0f,
.25f, .25f,
0f, .25f,
};
```

6.3 Change Sprite Sheet Frames

Problem

An image needs to change from one frame in the sprite sheet to another, rather than be static.

Solution

Move from one sprite sheet frame to another by translating the texture along the x and/or y axis.

How It Works

The glTranslatef() method is used in OpenGL ES 1 to translate or move a matrix within the coordinate system. To switch from the first frame in the sprite sheet to the second requires that you translate the texture matrix 25 percent along the x axis. (This is assuming you are using a sprite sheet that is set up like the one in Figure 6-2).

The first step is to put OpenGL ES into texture matrix mode, thus ensuring that you are modifying the texture's coordinates and not the vertices. The following code puts OpenGL ES into texture matrix mode, and maps the first frame of the sprite sheet (upper left-hand corner) onto the vertices.

```
gl.glMatrixMode(GL10.GL_TEXTURE);
gl.glLoadIdentity();
gl.glTranslatef(0f,.75f, 0f);
```

Notice that the y coordinate being passed to `glTranslatef()` is .75. On the coordinate scale of 0–1, .75 corresponds to the lower left-hand corner of the first row of frames in the sprite sheet. In this code sample, the x and y coordinates being passed to `glTranslatef()` are 0 and .75, respectively. Carrying this over to the image in Figure 6-4, (0, .75) is the lower left-hand corner of first frame on the first row of the sprite sheet. Figure 6.4 illustrates how the coordinates on the y axis line up with the sprite sheet.

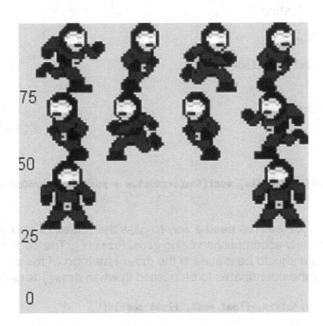

Figure 6-4. Sprite sheet with y-axis coordinates

If you want to change the texture that is mapped to your vertices to the second frame on the first row of the sprite sheet, use the `glTranslatef()` method to move the texture to (.25, .75). The x coordinate of .25 represents the lower left-hand corner on the x axis of the second frame on the first row.

```
gl.glMatrixMode(GL10.GL_TEXTURE);
gl.glLoadIdentity();
gl.glTranslatef(.25f,.75f, 0f);
```

If you are using OpenGL ES 2 or 3, the process for changing sprite sheet frames is different. You will need to add a pair of floats to your fragment shader. These floats will accept the x and y coordinate values for the position of the frame, much like `glTranslatef()`.

First, add the floats to the fragment shader code, as in Listing 6-4.

Listing 6-4. Adding floats to fragment shader code

```
private final String fragmentShaderCode =
"precisionmediump float;" +
"uniformvec4vColor;" +
"uniformsampler2DTexCoordIn;" +
```

```
"uniform float posX;" +
"uniform float posY;" +
"varyingvec2TexCoordOut;" +
"void main() {" +
"}";
```

Next, modify the main() method of the fragment shader to call texture2d() and pass it the values of posX and posY, as shown in Listing 6.5.

Listing 6-5. Modifying the main() method

```
private final String fragmentShaderCode =
"precisionmediump float;" +
"uniformvec4vColor;" +
"uniformsampler2DTexCoordIn;" +
"uniform float posX;" +
"uniform float posY;" +
"varyingvec2TexCoordOut;" +
"void main() {" +
" gl_FragColor = texture2D(TexCoordIn, vec2(TexCoordOut.x + posX,TexCoordOut.y + posY));"+
"}";
```

The shader code is now modified. You need a way to pass the values of posX and posY into the shader code. This is ultimately accomplished using glUniform1f(). The code to change the x and y position of the texture should be placed in the draw() method of the object's class. Modify the method signature to allow the coordinates to be passed in when draw() is called.

```
public void draw(float[] mvpMatrix, float posX, float posY) {
...
}
```

Use glGetUniformLocation() to get the location, in the shader, of the posX and posY floats, and then use glUniform1f() to assign new values, as shown in Listing 6-6.

Listing 6-6. draw()

```
public void draw(float[] mvpMatrix, float posX, float posY) {
GLES20.glUseProgram(mProgram);

mPositionHandle = GLES20.glGetAttribLocation(mProgram, "vPosition");

GLES20.glEnableVertexAttribArray(mPositionHandle);

intvsTextureCoord = GLES20.glGetAttribLocation(mProgram, "TexCoordIn");
GLES20.glVertexAttribPointer(mPositionHandle, COORDS_PER_VERTEX,
GLES20.GL_FLOAT, false,
vertexStride, vertexBuffer);
GLES20.glVertexAttribPointer(vsTextureCoord, COORDS_PER_TEXTURE,
GLES20.GL_FLOAT, false,
textureStride, textureBuffer);
GLES20.glEnableVertexAttribArray(vsTextureCoord);
GLES20.glActiveTexture(GLES20.GL_TEXTURE0);
```

```
GLES20.glBindTexture(GLES20.GL_TEXTURE_2D, textures[0]);
intfsTexture = GLES20.glGetUniformLocation(mProgram, "TexCoordOut");
intfsPosX = GLES20.glGetUniformLocation(mProgram, "posX");
intfsPosY = GLES20.glGetUniformLocation(mProgram, "posY");
GLES20.glUniform1i(fsTexture, 0);
GLES20.glUniform1f(fsPosX, posX);
GLES20.glUniform1f(fsPosY, posY);
mMVPMatrixHandle = GLES20.glGetUniformLocation(mProgram, "uMVPMatrix");

GLES20.glUniformMatrix4fv(mMVPMatrixHandle, 1, false, mvpMatrix, 0);

GLES20.glDrawElements(GLES20.GL_TRIANGLES, drawOrder.length,
GLES20.GL_UNSIGNED_SHORT, drawListBuffer);

GLES20.glDisableVertexAttribArray(mPositionHandle);
}
```

6.4 Animate Images from a Sprite Sheet

Problem

An image needs to be an animation that changes over time (as if the character is running).

Solution

Flip through multiple sprite sheet images in a specific order.

How It Works

In this solution, you are going to build on the uses of the glTranslatef() and glUnifor1f() methods from the previous solution. The glTranslatef() method, for OpenGL ES 1, has been shown to move the mapped texture on the vertices so that only specific portions of the sprite sheet are visible. If you perform this action fast enough, and with enough frames, you will have animation.

For this solution, you once again use the sprite sheet shown in Figure 6-2. This solution also builds on Chapter 5,"Reading Player Input."

Create an enumeration that can be set when the player touches either the right or left sides on the screen, indicating that the character should run to the right or left, respectively (see Listing 6-7).

These variables should be placed so that you can access them both from the renderer and from the main Activity.

Listing 6-7. Updating Player Movement

```
public static intplayerAction = 0;
public static final int PLAYER_MOVE_LEFT = 1;
public static final int PLAYER_STAND = 0;
public static final int PLAYER_MOVE_RIGHT = 2;
```

You also need to set up six more variables (Listing 6-8).

Listing 6-8. Setting up six more variables

```
public static float playerCurrentLocation  = .75f;
public static float currentRunAniFrame  = 0f;
public static float currentStandingFrame  = 0f;

public static final float PLAYER_RUN_SPEED = .25f;
public static final float STANDING_LEFT = 0f;
public static final float STANDING_RIGHT = .75f;
```

playerCurrentLocation is used to track the current location of the sprite on the screen. currentRunAniFrame is used to track the current frame of animation from the sprite sheet, which is making the character appear to run. Like currentRunAniFrame, currentStandingFrame is used to track which frame of the sprite sheet is being used to make the character appear to be standing.

PLAYER_RUN_SPEED will be used to move the sprite across the screen at specific intervals. Combined with the animation, PLAYER_RUN_SPEED is used to give the illusion that the character is actually running. Finally, the STANDING_LEFT and STANDING_RIGHT variables hold the value that represents the lower left corner on the x axis of the two frames from the sprite sheet that represent the character standing. One frame is facing left and the other is facing right.

Referring back to Chapter 5, Listing 6-9 sets the playerAction based on whether the player has touched the right or the left side of the screen. The onTouchEvent for the game's main Activity has been modified to set the playerAction to either PLAYER_MOVE_RIGHT, PLAYER_MOVE_LEFT, or PLAYER_STAND.

Listing 6-9. onTouchEvent()

```
@Override
publicbooleanonTouchEvent(MotionEvent event) {
float x = event.getX();
float y = event.getY();
DisplayMetricsoutMetrics = new DisplayMetrics();

display.getMetrics(outMetrics);

int height = outMetrics.heightPixels / 4;

int playableArea = outMetrics.heightPixels - height;
if (y >playableArea){
switch (event.getAction()){
case MotionEvent.ACTION_DOWN:
if(x <outMetrics.widthPixels / 2){
playerAction = PLAYER_MOVE_RIGHT;
}else{
playerAction = PLAYER_MOVE_LEFT;
}
break;
case MotionEvent.ACTION_UP:
playerAction = PLAYER_STAND;
break;
}
}

return false;
}
```

Next, set up a case statement to read the value of playerAction. The game loop is contained within the onDraw() method of the Renderer. This method is executed on a constant loop. Therefore, you can create a new method in the Renderer named movePlayer() and call it from the onDraw() method of the Renderer.

Every time the onDraw() method executes, it will call movePlayer(). All you need to do in the movePlayer() method is tell OpenGL ES how you would like flip through the sprite sheet and "move" the character.

First, create the movePlayer() method and set up a case statement to iterate though the playerAction. In the code shown in Listing 6-10, goodguy refers to an instantiation of the SuperBanditGuy class. This could represent whatever class you are using in your game.

Listing 6-10. movePlayer()

```
private void movePlayer(GL10gl){
if(!goodguy.isDead)
{
switch(playeraction){
case PLAYER_MOVE_RIGHT:

break;

case PLAYER_MOVE_LEFT:

break;

case PLAYER_STAND:

break;
}
}
}
```

In Recipe 6.3, you learned how to use the glTranslatef() and glUniform1f() methods to move from one frame of sprite sheet to another. The only difference in this solution is that you will be automating the process. This means that because onDraw(), and thereby movePlayer(), is called on a loop, you must write the call to glTranslatef() in such a way that it will automatically cycle from one frame to the next each time it is called. Listings 6-11 and 6-12 show what this code looks like when you want to move the character to the right, using both OpenGL ES 1 and OpenGL ES 2/3.

Listing 6-11. Moving the Frame with the Player (OpenGLES 1)

```
currentStandingFrame    = STANDING_RIGHT;
playerCurrentLocation  += PLAYER_RUN_SPEED;

currentRunAniFrame  += .25t;
if (currentRunAniFrame> .75f)
{
currentRunAniFrame  = .0f;
}
```

```
gl.glMatrixMode(GL10.GL_MODELVIEW);
gl.glLoadIdentity();
gl.glPushMatrix();
gl.glScalef(.15f, .15f, 1f);
gl.glTranslatef(playercurrentlocation, .75f, 0f);
gl.glMatrixMode(GL10.GL_TEXTURE);
gl.glLoadIdentity();
gl.glTranslatef(currentRunAniFrame,.75f, 0.0f);
goodguy.draw(gl,spritesheets,SBG_RUNNING_PTR);
gl.glPopMatrix();
gl.glLoadIdentity();
```

Listing 6-12. Moving the Frame with the Player (OpenGL ES 2/3)

```
currentStandingFrame    = STANDING_RIGHT;
playerCurrentLocation   += PLAYER_RUN_SPEED;

currentRunAniFrame   += .25f;
if (currentRunAniFrame> .75f)
{
currentRunAniFrame   = .0f;
}

goodguy.draw(mMVPMatrix, currentRunAniFrame, .75f );
```

First, because the character is running to the right, when he stops running he should be facing right. Therefore, the currentStandingFrame is set to STANDING_RIGHT. Then, the PLAYER_RUN_SPEED is added to the playercurrentlocation,resulting in a value that is .25 away from the original location. When this is rendered, the sprite is moved to the new location.

The next block keeps the animation loop moving. Your sprite sheet has four images with the lower left corners at 0, .25, .50, and .75, respectively, on the x axis. To achieve a smooth animation, you are going to start with the first frame (0) and add .25 to get to the second frame, and so on. When you reach the last frame of animation (.75), you need to start over again at 0. An if() statement checks whether you are at the last frame of animation, and resets you back to the first.

Finally, OpenGL is used to draw the new frame of animation. Notice that glTranslatef() is called twice—once in model matrix mode, and once in texture matrix mode. When it is called in model matrix mode, it moves the physical location of the vertices that your texture is mapped to, thus moving the character to the right. When glTranslatef() is called in texture matrix mode, the frame of animation is advanced.

Listings 6-13 and 6-14 show the finished movePlayer() method, again using both OpenGL ES 1 and OpenGL ES 2/3.

Listing 6-13. Completed movePlayer() (OpenGL ES 1)

```
private void movePlayer(GL10gl){
if(!goodguy.isDead)
{
switch(playeraction){
case PLAYER_MOVE_RIGHT:
currentStandingFrame    = STANDING_RIGHT;
```

```
playerCurrentLocation  += PLAYER_RUN_SPEED;
currentRunAniFrame  += .25f;
if (currentRunAniFrame> .75f)
{
currentRunAniFrame  = .0f;
}

gl.glMatrixMode(GL10.GL_MODELVIEW);
gl.glLoadIdentity();
gl.glPushMatrix();
gl.glScalef(.15f, .15f, 1f);
gl.glTranslatef(playerCurrentLocation, .75f, 0f);
gl.glMatrixMode(GL10.GL_TEXTURE);
gl.glLoadIdentity();
gl.glTranslatef(currentRunAniFrame,.75f, 0.0f);
goodguy.draw(gl,spritesheets,SBG_RUNNING_PTR);
gl.glPopMatrix();
gl.glLoadIdentity();

break;

case PLAYER_MOVE_LEFT:
currentStandingFrame  = STANDING_LEFT;
playerCurrentLocation  -= PLAYER_RUN_SPEED;
currentRunAniFrame  += .25f;
if (currentRunAniFrame> .75f)
{
currentRunAniFrame  = .0f;
}

gl.glMatrixMode(GL10.GL_MODELVIEW);
gl.glLoadIdentity();
gl.glPushMatrix();
gl.glScalef(.15f, .15f, 1f);
gl.glTranslatef(playerCurrentLocation, .75f, 0f);
gl.glMatrixMode(GL10.GL_TEXTURE);
gl.glLoadIdentity();
gl.glTranslatef(currentRunAniFrame,.50f, 0.0f);
goodguy.draw(gl,spritesheets,SBG_RUNNING_PTR);
gl.glPopMatrix();
gl.glLoadIdentity();

break;

case PLAYER_STAND:
gl.glMatrixMode(GL10.GL_MODELVIEW);
gl.glLoadIdentity();
gl.glPushMatrix();
gl.glScalef(.15f, .15f, 1f);
gl.glTranslatef(playerCurrentLocation, .75f, 0f);
gl.glMatrixMode(GL10.GL_TEXTURE);
gl.glLoadIdentity();
```

```
gl.glTranslatef(currentStandingFrame,.25f, 0.0f);
goodguy.draw(gl,spritesheets,SBG_RUNNING_PTR);
gl.glPopMatrix();
gl.glLoadIdentity();
break;
}
}
}
```

Listing 6-14. Completed movePlayer() (OpenGL ES 2/3)

```
private void movePlayer(GL10gl){
if(!goodguy.isDead)
{
switch(playeraction){
case PLAYER_MOVE_RIGHT:
currentStandingFrame   = STANDING_RIGHT;
playerCurrentLocation  += PLAYER_RUN_SPEED;
currentRunAniFrame  += .25f;
if (currentRunAniFrame> .75f)
{
currentRunAniFrame  = .0f;
}

goodguy.draw(mMVPMatrix, currentRunAniFrame, .75f );
break;

case PLAYER_MOVE_LEFT:
currentStandingFrame   = STANDING_LEFT;
playerCurrentLocation  -= PLAYER_RUN_SPEED;
currentRunAniFrame  += .25f;
if (currentRunAniFrame> .75f)
{
currentRunAniFrame  = .0f;
}

goodguy.draw(mMVPMatrix, currentRunAniFrame, .50f );
break;

case PLAYER_STAND:
goodguy.draw(mMVPMatrix, currentStandingFrame, .25f );
break;
}
}
}
```

Chapter 7

Scrolling a Background

The solutions in this chapter will help you create a scrolling background for a game. Many game types have background images that scroll as the player is playing. Chances are you have some questions about just how to make the background image of your game appear to move.

In some cases, the images will scroll automatically. For example, scrolling shooters and other "rail"-style games will have backgrounds that scroll automatically. This is in contrast to other game types, such as side-scrolling platform games, where the background image will scroll in coordination with the movements of the player (this is covered in Chapter 8, "Scrolling Multiple Backgrounds").

This chapter will present three solutions for loading the background image, scrolling that image vertically, and scrolling that image horizontally.

7.1 Load the Background Image
Problem

Your game cannot load a background image using OpenGL ES.

Solution

Create a class that can load the image as a texture and map it to a set of vertices.

How It Works

The easiest way to load an image for use by OpenGL ES, is to create a custom class that creates all of the vertices required and maps the image as a texture to those vertices. Because this background is going to scroll, the class also needs to map the texture in a way that it will be able to repeat itself. The background image will appear as though it goes on infinitely, if OpenGL ES can repeat the texture as it scrolls.

One of the most common types of backgrounds used to scroll infinitely, and one of the easiest to work with, is a star field. Star fields are random patterns of dots that are easy to repeat seamlessly. Games such as side-scrolling shooters often use star fields as an infinitely scrolling background.

Figure 7-1 illustrates the star field image that will be used in this solution.

Figure 7-1. A star field image

The first step is to add the image to the correct `res/drawable` folder of your project. We've already discussed adding images to a project, and the various folders available for this purpose (see Chapter 2, "Loading and Image," Chapter 3, "The Splash Screen," or Chapter 6, "Loading a Sprite Sheet," for more specific information). After the image file has been added to the project, create a new class. For this solution, the name of the new class will be SBGBackground().

```
public class SBGBackground {

}
```

A similar class was created in Chapter 6 to load the image and vertices for a spritesheet character. Much of the code for Listings 7-1 (for OpenGL ES 1) and 7-2 (for OpenGL ES 2/3) come directly from the solution in Chapter 6.

Listing 7-1. SBGBackground()(OpenGL ES 1)

```
public class SBGBackground {

private FloatBuffer vertexBuffer;
private FloatBuffer textureBuffer;
private ByteBuffer indexBuffer;
```

```java
private int[] textures = new int[1];

private float vertices[] = {
0.0f, 0.0f, 0.0f,
1.0f, 0.0f, 0.0f,
1.0f, 1.0f, 0.0f,
0.0f, 1.0f, 0.0f,
};

private float texture[] = {
0.0f, 0.0f,
1.0f, 0f,
1f, 1.0f,
0f, 1f,
};

private byte indices[] = {
0,1,2,
0,2,3,
};

public SBGBackground() {
    ByteBuffer byteBuf = ByteBuffer.allocateDirect(vertices.length * 4);
byteBuf.order(ByteOrder.nativeOrder());
vertexBuffer = byteBuf.asFloatBuffer();
vertexBuffer.put(vertices);
vertexBuffer.position(0);

byteBuf = ByteBuffer.allocateDirect(texture.length * 4);
byteBuf.order(ByteOrder.nativeOrder());
textureBuffer = byteBuf.asFloatBuffer();
textureBuffer.put(texture);
textureBuffer.position(0);

indexBuffer = ByteBuffer.allocateDirect(indices.length);
indexBuffer.put(indices);
indexBuffer.position(0);
    }

public void draw(GL10 gl) {
gl.glBindTexture(GL10.GL_TEXTURE_2D, textures[0]);

gl.glFrontFace(GL10.GL_CCW);
gl.glEnable(GL10.GL_CULL_FACE);
gl.glCullFace(GL10.GL_BACK);

gl.glEnableClientState(GL10.GL_VERTEX_ARRAY);
gl.glEnableClientState(GL10.GL_TEXTURE_COORD_ARRAY);

gl.glVertexPointer(3, GL10.GL_FLOAT, 0, vertexBuffer);
gl.glTexCoordPointer(2, GL10.GL_FLOAT, 0, textureBuffer);
```

```
gl.glDrawElements(GL10.GL_TRIANGLES, indices.length, GL10.GL_UNSIGNED_BYTE, indexBuffer);

gl.glDisableClientState(GL10.GL_VERTEX_ARRAY);
gl.glDisableClientState(GL10.GL_TEXTURE_COORD_ARRAY);
gl.glDisable(GL10.GL_CULL_FACE);
    }
}
```

Listing 7-2. SBGBackground()(OpenGL ES 2/3)

```
class SBGBackground{
private final String vertexShaderCode =
"uniform mat4 uMVPMatrix;" +
"attribute vec4 vPosition;" +
"attribute vec2 TexCoordIn;" +
"varying vec2 TexCoordOut;" +
"void main() {" +
"  gl_Position = uMVPMatrix * vPosition;" +
"  TexCoordOut = TexCoordIn;" +
"}";

private final String fragmentShaderCode =
"precision mediump float;" +
"uniform vec4 vColor;" +
"uniform sampler2D TexCoordIn;" +
"uniform float scroll;" +
"varying vec2 TexCoordOut;" +
"void main() {" +
"}";
private float texture[] = {
 0f, 0f,
.25f, 0f,
.25f, .25f,
0f, .25f,
};

private int[] textures = new int[1];
private final FloatBuffer vertexBuffer;
private final ShortBuffer drawListBuffer;
private final FloatBuffer textureBuffer;
private final int mProgram;
private int mPositionHandle;
private int mMVPMatrixHandle;

static final int COORDS_PER_VERTEX = 3;
static final int COORDS_PER_TEXTURE = 2;
static float squareCoords[] = { -1f,  1f, 0.0f,
-1f, -1f, 0.0f,
1f, -1f, 0.0f,
1f,  1f, 0.0f };
```

```
private final short drawOrder[] = { 0, 1, 2, 0, 2, 3 };

private final int vertexStride = COORDS_PER_VERTEX * 4;
public static int textureStride = COORDS_PER_TEXTURE * 4;

public SBGBackground() {
ByteBuffer bb = ByteBuffer.allocateDirect(
bb.order(ByteOrder.nativeOrder());
vertexBuffer = bb.asFloatBuffer();
vertexBuffer.put(squareCoords);
vertexBuffer.position(0);

bb = ByteBuffer.allocateDirect(texture.length * 4);
bb.order(ByteOrder.nativeOrder());
textureBuffer = bb.asFloatBuffer();
textureBuffer.put(texture);
textureBuffer.position(0);

ByteBuffer dlb = ByteBuffer.allocateDirect(
dlb.order(ByteOrder.nativeOrder());
drawListBuffer = dlb.asShortBuffer();
drawListBuffer.put(drawOrder);
drawListBuffer.position(0);

int vertexShader = SBGGameRenderer.loadShader(
GLES20.GL_VERTEX_SHADER,vertexShaderCode);
int fragmentShader = SBGGameRenderer.loadShader(
GLES20.GL_FRAGMENT_SHADER,fragmentShaderCode);

mProgram = GLES20.glCreateProgram();
GLES20.glAttachShader(mProgram, vertexShader);
GLES20.glAttachShader(mProgram, fragmentShader);
GLES20.glLinkProgram(mProgram);
}

public void draw(float[] mvpMatrix) {
GLES20.glUseProgram(mProgram);

mPositionHandle = GLES20.glGetAttribLocation(mProgram, "vPosition");

GLES20.glEnableVertexAttribArray(mPositionHandle);

int vsTextureCoord = GLES20.glGetAttribLocation(mProgram, "TexCoordIn");
GLES20.glVertexAttribPointer(
mPositionHandle, COORDS_PER_VERTEX,
GLES20.GL_FLOAT, false,
vertexStride, vertexBuffer);
GLES20.glVertexAttribPointer(vsTextureCoord, COORDS_PER_TEXTURE,
GLES20.GL_FLOAT, false,
textureStride, textureBuffer);
GLES20.glEnableVertexAttribArray(vsTextureCoord);
GLES20.glActiveTexture(GLES20.GL_TEXTURE0);
```

```
GLES20.glBindTexture(GLES20.GL_TEXTURE_2D, textures[0]);
int fsTexture = GLES20.glGetUniformLocation(mProgram, "TexCoordOut");
GLES20.glUniform1i(fsTexture, 0);
mMVPMatrixHandle = GLES20.glGetUniformLocation(mProgram, "uMVPMatrix");

GLES20.glUniformMatrix4fv(mMVPMatrixHandle, 1, false, mvpMatrix, 0);

GLES20.glDrawElements(GLES20.GL_TRIANGLES, drawOrder.length,
GLES20.GL_UNSIGNED_SHORT, drawListBuffer);

GLES20.glDisableVertexAttribArray(mPositionHandle);
}
}
```

This class, in its current form, creates vertex, index, and texture arrays. It also contains a constructor that initializes the buffers and a draw() method that is called when the background image needs to be drawn. This class should look substantially familiar, based on other image classes you've seen from previous solutions in this book.

Take special note of the bolded line of code in Listing 7-1. This line creates an int array named textures, but only instantiates it to one element. The reason for this is that an existing OpenGL ES method used to generate texture names (glGenTextures) only accepts an array of textures, as it was built to work on multiple textures.

Now we'll create a new method named loadTexture() using both OpenGL ES 1 and OpenGL ES 2/3, which is needed to load the image file and map it as a texture to the vertices. For OpenGL ES 1, use the following:

```
public void loadTexture(GL10 gl,int texture, Context context) {

}
```

For OpenGL ES 2/3, use the following:

```
public void loadTexture(int texture, Context context) {

}
```

Notice that the OpenGL ES 1 version of the method accepts an OpenGL ES object, the ID of the image to load, and the current Android context. Within this method, you need to create a bitmap from the image (using the ID that is passed in) and then set some texture parameters that will dictate how OpenGL ES treats the texture (see Listings 7-3 and 7-4).

Listing 7-3. loadTexture() (OpenGL ES 1)

```
public void loadTexture(GL10 gl,int texture, Context context) {
InputStream imagestream = context.getResources().openRawResource(texture);
Bitmap bitmap = null;
```

```
try {

bitmap = BitmapFactory.decodeStream(imagestream);

}catch(Exception e){

}finally {
try {
imagestream.close();
imagestream = null;
} catch (IOException e) {
}
}

gl.glGenTextures(1, textures, 0);
gl.glBindTexture(GL10.GL_TEXTURE_2D, textures[0]);

gl.glTexParameterf(GL10.GL_TEXTURE_2D, GL10.GL_TEXTURE_MIN_FILTER, GL10.GL_NEAREST);
gl.glTexParameterf(GL10.GL_TEXTURE_2D, GL10.GL_TEXTURE_MAG_FILTER, GL10.GL_LINEAR);

gl.glTexParameterf(GL10.GL_TEXTURE_2D, GL10.GL_TEXTURE_WRAP_S, GL10.GL_REPEAT);
gl.glTexParameterf(GL10.GL_TEXTURE_2D, GL10.GL_TEXTURE_WRAP_T, GL10.GL_REPEAT);

GLUtils.texImage2D(GL10.GL_TEXTURE_2D, 0, bitmap, 0);

bitmap.recycle();
}
```

Listing 7-4. loadTexture()(OpenGL ES 2/3)

```
public void loadTexture(int texture, Context context) {
InputStream imagestream = context.getResources().openRawResource(texture);
Bitmap bitmap = null;

android.graphics.Matrix flip = new android.graphics.Matrix();
flip.postScale(-1f, -1f);

try {

bitmap = BitmapFactory.decodeStream(imagestream);

}catch(Exception e){
//Handle your exceptions here
}finally {
try {
imagestream.close();
imagestream = null;
} catch (IOException e) {
 //Handle your exceptions here
}
}
```

```
GLES20.glGenTextures(1, textures, 0);
GLES20.glBindTexture(GLES20.GL_TEXTURE_2D, textures[0]);

GLES20.glTexParameterf(GLES20.GL_TEXTURE_2D, GLES20.GL_TEXTURE_MIN_FILTER, GLES20.GL_NEAREST);
GLES20.glTexParameterf(GLES20.GL_TEXTURE_2D, GLES20.GL_TEXTURE_MAG_FILTER, GLES20.GL_LINEAR);

GLES20.glTexParameterf(GLES20.GL_TEXTURE_2D, GLES20.GL_TEXTURE_WRAP_S, GLES20.GL_REPEAT);
GLES20.glTexParameterf(GLES20.GL_TEXTURE_2D, GLES20.GL_TEXTURE_WRAP_T, GLES20.GL_REPEAT);

GLUtils.texImage2D(GLES20.GL_TEXTURE_2D, 0, bitmap, 0);

bitmap.recycle();
}
```

Pay particular attention to the bolded code in this method. This code explicitly sets the texture to repeat along the x and y axes. In OpenGL ES, the S texture coordinate axis refers to the x Cartesian axis; T refers to the y axis. Repeating the texture is critical in this example because we are using one star field image that will be repeated infinitely.

Now that the SBGBackground() class is complete, there is code that needs to be added to the game loop that utilizes the new class. There are two more steps to completing this solution. The first is to instantiate a new SBGBackground. Then the image ID must be passed to the loadTexture() method.

In your game loop, instantiate a new SBGBackground, as follows:

```
private SBGBackground background1 = new SBGBackground();
```

The game loop is contained in an implementation of an OpenGL ES Renderer. As such, it has some required methods that, again, were covered heavily in previous chapters. One of these methods is onSurfaceCreated(), and this is where the code for loading the texture should be called.

```
public void onSurfaceCreated(GL10 gl, EGLConfig config) {
//TODO Auto-generated method stub

...

background1.loadTexture(gl, R.drawable.starfield, context);
}
```

The next two solutions will cover scrolling the background texture now that it has been loaded.

7.2 Scroll the Background Horizontally
Problem
The background is currently static, and it should scroll horizontally.

Solution
Create a new class in the game loop that translates the background texture a set amount on the y axis.

How It Works

The first step in the OpenGL ES 1 version of this solution is to create two variables that will be used to track the current location of the background texture and the value by which to translate the texture, respectively.

```
int bgScroll1 = 0;
float SCROLL_BACKGROUND_1 = .002f;
```

These variables can be local to your Renderer class, or you can store them in a separate class.

The onDrawFrame() method, within an implementation of an OpenGL ES Renderer, is called on every iteration of the game loop. You need to create a new method, called scrollBackground(), that is in turn called from the onDrawFrame() method (see Listing 7-5).

Listing 7-5. scrollBackground() (OpenGL ES 1)

```
private void scrollBackground1(GL10 gl){
if (bgScroll1 == Float.MAX_VALUE){
bgScroll1 = 0f;
}

gl.glMatrixMode(GL10.GL_MODELVIEW);
gl.glLoadIdentity();
gl.glPushMatrix();
gl.glScalef(1f, 1f, 1f);
gl.glTranslatef(0f, 0f, 0f);

gl.glMatrixMode(GL10.GL_TEXTURE);
gl.glLoadIdentity();
gl.glTranslatef(0.0f, bgScroll1, 0.0f);

background1.draw(gl);
gl.glPopMatrix();
bgScroll1 +=  SCROLL_BACKGROUND_1;
gl.glLoadIdentity();

}
```

The first part of this method tests the current value of the bgScroll1 variable. Given that floats have an upper limit, this if statement is necessary to insure you do not overload your float.

Next, the model matrix view is scaled and translated before you begin to work with the texture matrix. Notice that the y coordinate of the texture model is translated by the value in bgScroll1. This is what moves your background across the screen.

Finally, the draw() method of the SBGBackground() class is called, and the bgScroll1 variable is incremented by the value in the SCROLL_BACKGROUND_1 variable to prepare for the next iteration of the loop.

Call the new scrollBackground() method from the onDrawFrame() method and the background star field will move smoothly across the screen horizontally.

Accomplishing this same process in OpenGL ES 2/3 is slightly different (see Listing 7-6). The variable for controlling the scroll is setup in the draw() method of the object class. This variable can also be passed into the draw() method, like that used for the spritesheet solution in Chapter 6. However, since this background is scrolling automatically, and infinitely, it makes more sense to handle everything in the method.

Listing 7-6. scrollBackground() (OpenGL ES 2/3)

```
class SBGBackground{
public float scroll = 0;
private final String vertexShaderCode =
"uniform mat4 uMVPMatrix;" +
"attribute vec4 vPosition;" +
"attribute vec2 TexCoordIn;" +
"varying vec2 TexCoordOut;" +
"void main() {" +
"  gl_Position = uMVPMatrix * vPosition;" +
"  TexCoordOut = TexCoordIn;" +
"}";

private final String fragmentShaderCode =
"precision mediump float;" +
"uniform vec4 vColor;" +
"uniform sampler2D TexCoordIn;" +
"uniform float scroll;" +
"varying vec2 TexCoordOut;" +
"void main() {" +
" gl_FragColor = texture2D(TexCoordIn, vec2(TexCoordOut.x + scroll,TexCoordOut.y));"+
"}";
private float texture[] = {
0f, 0f,
.25f, 0f,
.25f, .25f,
0f, .25f,
};

private int[] textures = new int[1];
private final FloatBuffer vertexBuffer;
private final ShortBuffer drawListBuffer;
private final FloatBuffer textureBuffer;
private final int mProgram;
private int mPositionHandle;
private int mMVPMatrixHandle;

static final int COORDS_PER_VERTEX = 3;
static final int COORDS_PER_TEXTURE = 2;
static float squareCoords[] = { -1f,  1f, 0.0f,
-1f, -1f, 0.0f,
1f, -1f, 0.0f,
1f,  1f, 0.0f };
```

```
private final short drawOrder[] = { 0, 1, 2, 0, 2, 3 };

private final int vertexStride = COORDS_PER_VERTEX * 4;
public static int textureStride = COORDS_PER_TEXTURE * 4;

public void loadTexture(int texture, Context context) {
    ...
  }
public SBGBackground() {
...
}


public void draw(float[] mvpMatrix) {
scroll += .01f;
GLES20.glUseProgram(mProgram);

mPositionHandle = GLES20.glGetAttribLocation(mProgram, "vPosition");

GLES20.glEnableVertexAttribArray(mPositionHandle);

int vsTextureCoord = GLES20.glGetAttribLocation(mProgram, "TexCoordIn");
GLES20.glVertexAttribPointer(mPositionHandle, COORDS_PER_VERTEX,
GLES20.GL_FLOAT, false,
vertexStride, vertexBuffer);
GLES20.glVertexAttribPointer(vsTextureCoord, COORDS_PER_TEXTURE,
GLES20.GL_FLOAT, false,
textureStride, textureBuffer);
GLES20.glEnableVertexAttribArray(vsTextureCoord);
GLES20.glActiveTexture(GLES20.GL_TEXTURE0);
GLES20.glBindTexture(GLES20.GL_TEXTURE_2D, textures[0]);
int fsTexture = GLES20.glGetUniformLocation(mProgram, "TexCoordOut");
int fsScroll = GLES20.glGetUniformLocation(mProgram, "scroll");
GLES20.glUniform1i(fsTexture, 0);
GLES20.glUniform1f(fsScroll, scroll);
mMVPMatrixHandle = GLES20.glGetUniformLocation(mProgram, "uMVPMatrix");

GLES20.glUniformMatrix4fv(mMVPMatrixHandle, 1, false, mvpMatrix, 0);

GLES20.glDrawElements(GLES20.GL_TRIANGLES, drawOrder.length,
GLES20.GL_UNSIGNED_SHORT, drawListBuffer);

GLES20.glDisableVertexAttribArray(mPositionHandle);
}
}
```

7.3 Scroll the Background Vertically

Problem

The background is currently static, and it should scroll horizontally.

Solution

Create a new class in the game loop that translates the background texture a set amount on the x axis.

How It Works

Building on the previous solution, only one change needs to be made to scroll the background vertically rather than horizontally, as shown in Listings 7-7 and 7-8.

Listing 7-7. Vertical Scroll (OpenGL ES 1)

```
private void scrollBackground1(GL10 gl){
if (bgScroll1 == Float.MAX_VALUE){
bgScroll1 = 0f;
}

gl.glMatrixMode(GL10.GL_MODELVIEW);
gl.glLoadIdentity();
gl.glPushMatrix();
gl.glScalef(1f, 1f, 1f);
gl.glTranslatef(0f, 0f, 0f);

gl.glMatrixMode(GL10.GL_TEXTURE);
gl.glLoadIdentity();
gl.glTranslatef(bgScroll1, 0.0f, 0.0f);

background1.draw(gl);
gl.glPopMatrix();
bgScroll1 +=   SCROLL_BACKGROUND_1;
gl.glLoadIdentity();

}
```

Listing 7-8. Vertical Scroll (OpenGL ES 2/3)

```
private final String fragmentShaderCode =
"precision mediump float;" +
"uniform vec4 vColor;" +
"uniform sampler2D TexCoordIn;" +
"uniform float scroll;" +
"varying vec2 TexCoordOut;" +
"void main() {" +
" gl_FragColor = texture2D(TexCoordIn, vec2(TexCoordOut.x,TexCoordOut.y+ scroll));"+
"}";
```

Notice the bolded code in the scrollBackground() for OpenGL ES 1 method. The bgScroll1 value has been moved from the y axis position to the x axis position in the glTranslatef() method call. This is all that is needed to cause the background to scroll vertically rather than horizontally.

The only code that needs to be changed for OpenGL ES 2/3 is the fragment shader. The scroll float is now added to the y coordinate of the texture rather than the x.

Chapter 8

Scrolling Multiple Backgrounds

In Chapter 7, solutions were presented for creating a background that could scroll. While that solution will help you create a compelling looking game, it could have more depth.

In this chapter, you will be presented with solutions for loading and using two images in your game's background. Not only will this make your game more dynamic, it will allow you to scroll the two images at different speeds.

At the end of this chapter, a solution is presented for scrolling two different background images at different speeds. This gives a game a more realistic look and it adds depth to an otherwise flat environment.

8.1 Load Two Background Images

Problem

The background of the game needs to contain two images.

Solution

Use OpenGL to load two images to create a layered background that can be scrolled independently for a more dynamic look.

How It Works

As discussed in Chapter 7, the easiest way to load an image for use by OpenGL ES, is to create a custom class that loads all of the vertices required and maps the image as a texture to those vertices.

In this solution, you will copy two images into the res folder of your project. Then, you will instantiate two copies of the class created for the solutions in Chapter 7. Using these two separate instantiations, you will then load up and draw two different images in the background. Figures 8-1 and 8-2 illustrate the star field image and the debris field image that will be used in this solution.

Figure 8-1. *Thestar field image*

Figure 8-2. *The debris field image*

The first step is to add the images to the correct res/drawable folder of your project. We've previously discussed adding images to a project, and the various folders available for this purpose. After the image files have been added to the project, you can instantiate two copies of the class that was created in Chapter 7.

The classes need to be instantiated in the class containing the game loop. The class containing the game loop is an implementation of an OpenGL ES Renderer. The background classes should be instantiated in a location that all of the methods of the Renderer have access to.

For reference, Listings 8-1 and 8-2 show the completed code of the SBGBackground() class from Chapter 7.

Listing 8-1. SBGBackground (OpenGL ES 1)

```
public class SBGBackground {

private FloatBuffer vertexBuffer;
private FloatBuffer textureBuffer;
private ByteBuffer indexBuffer;

private int[] textures = new int[1];

private float vertices[] = {
0.0f, 0.0f, 0.0f,
1.0f, 0.0f, 0.0f,
1.0f, 1.0f, 0.0f,
0.0f, 1.0f, 0.0f,
};

private float texture[] = {
0.0f, 0.0f,
1.0f, 0f,
1f, 1.0f,
0f, 1f,
};

private byte indices[] = {
0,1,2,
0,2,3,
};

Public SBGBackground() {
ByteBuffer byteBuf = ByteBuffer.allocateDirect(vertices.length * 4);
byteBuf.order(ByteOrder.nativeOrder());
vertexBuffer = byteBuf.asFloatBuffer();
vertexBuffer.put(vertices);
vertexBuffer.position(0);

byteBuf = ByteBuffer.allocateDirect(texture.length * 4);
byteBuf.order(ByteOrder.nativeOrder());
textureBuffer = byteBuf.asFloatBuffer();
textureBuffer.put(texture);
textureBuffer.position(0);

indexBuffer = ByteBuffer.allocateDirect(indices.length);
indexBuffer.put(indices);
indexBuffer.position(0);
    }

public void draw(GL10gl) {
gl.glBindTexture(GL10.GL_TEXTURE_2D, textures[0]);
```

```
gl.glFrontFace(GL10.GL_CCW);
gl.glEnable(GL10.GL_CULL_FACE);
gl.glCullFace(GL10.GL_BACK);

gl.glEnableClientState(GL10.GL_VERTEX_ARRAY);
gl.glEnableClientState(GL10.GL_TEXTURE_COORD_ARRAY);

gl.glVertexPointer(3, GL10.GL_FLOAT, 0, vertexBuffer);
gl.glTexCoordPointer(2, GL10.GL_FLOAT, 0, textureBuffer);

gl.glDrawElements(GL10.GL_TRIANGLES, indices.length, GL10.GL_UNSIGNED_BYTE, indexBuffer);

gl.glDisableClientState(GL10.GL_VERTEX_ARRAY);
gl.glDisableClientState(GL10.GL_TEXTURE_COORD_ARRAY);
gl.glDisable(GL10.GL_CULL_FACE);
    }

public void loadTexture(GL10gl,int texture, Context context) {
InputStream imagestream = context.getResources().openRawResource(texture);
Bitmap bitmap = null;
try {

bitmap = BitmapFactory.decodeStream(imagestream);

}catch(Exception e){

}finally {
try {
imagestream.close();
imagestream = null;
} catch (IOException e) {
}
}

gl.glGenTextures(1, textures, 0);
gl.glBindTexture(GL10.GL_TEXTURE_2D, textures[0]);

gl.glTexParameterf(GL10.GL_TEXTURE_2D, GL10.GL_TEXTURE_MIN_FILTER, GL10.GL_NEAREST);
gl.glTexParameterf(GL10.GL_TEXTURE_2D, GL10.GL_TEXTURE_MAG_FILTER, GL10.GL_LINEAR);

gl.glTexParameterf(GL10.GL_TEXTURE_2D, GL10.GL_TEXTURE_WRAP_S, GL10.GL_REPEAT);
gl.glTexParameterf(GL10.GL_TEXTURE_2D, GL10.GL_TEXTURE_WRAP_T, GL10.GL_REPEAT);

GLUtils.texImage2D(GL10.GL_TEXTURE_2D, 0, bitmap, 0);

bitmap.recycle();
}

}
```

Listing 8-2. SBGBackground (OpenGL ES 2/3)

```
class SBGBackground{
private final String vertexShaderCode =
"uniform mat4 uMVPMatrix;" +
"attribute vec4 vPosition;" +
"attribute vec2 TexCoordIn;" +
"varying vec2 TexCoordOut;" +
"void main() {" +
"  gl_Position = uMVPMatrix * vPosition;" +
"  TexCoordOut = TexCoordIn;" +
"}";

private final String fragmentShaderCode =
"precision mediump float;" +
"uniform vec4 vColor;" +
"uniform sampler2D TexCoordIn;" +
"uniform float scroll;" +
"varying vec2 TexCoordOut;" +
"void main() {" +
" gl_FragColor = texture2D(TexCoordIn, vec2(TexCoordOut.x + scroll,TexCoordOut.y));"+
"}";
private float texture[] = {
Of, Of,
.25f, Of,
.25f, .25f,
Of, .25f,
};

Private int[] textures = new int[1];
private final FloatBuffer vertexBuffer;
private final ShortBuffer drawListBuffer;
private final FloatBuffer textureBuffer;
private final int mProgram;
private int mPositionHandle;
private int mMVPMatrixHandle;

static final int COORDS_PER_VERTEX = 3;
static final int COORDS_PER_TEXTURE = 2;
static float squareCoords[] = { -1f,  1f, 0.0f,
 -1f, -1f, 0.0f,
1f, -1f, 0.0f,
1f,  1f, 0.0f };

private final short drawOrder[] = { 0, 1, 2, 0, 2, 3 };

private final int vertexStride = COORDS_PER_VERTEX * 4;
public static int textureStride = COORDS_PER_TEXTURE * 4;

public void loadTexture(int texture, Context context) {
InputStreami magestream = context.getResources().openRawResource(texture);
      Bitmap bitmap = null;
```

```java
android.graphics.Matrix flip = new android.graphics.Matrix();
flip.postScale(-1f, -1f);
try {

bitmap = BitmapFactory.decodeStream(imagestream);

}catch(Exception e){

}finally {
try {
imagestream.close();
imagestream = null;
} catch (IOException e) {
}
        }

GLES20.glGenTextures(1, textures, 0);
GLES20.glBindTexture(GLES20.GL_TEXTURE_2D, textures[0]);

GLES20.glTexParameterf(GLES20.GL_TEXTURE_2D, GLES20.GL_TEXTURE_MIN_FILTER,
GLES20.GL_NEAREST);
GLES20.glTexParameterf(GLES20.GL_TEXTURE_2D, GLES20.GL_TEXTURE_MAG_FILTER,
GLES20.GL_LINEAR);

GLES20.glTexParameterf(GLES20.GL_TEXTURE_2D, GLES20.GL_TEXTURE_WRAP_S, GLES20.GL_REPEAT);
GLES20.glTexParameterf(GLES20.GL_TEXTURE_2D, GLES20.GL_TEXTURE_WRAP_T, GLES20.GL_REPEAT);

GLUtils.texImage2D(GLES20.GL_TEXTURE_2D, 0, bitmap, 0);

bitmap.recycle();
    }
public SBGBackground() {
ByteBuffer bb = ByteBuffer.allocateDirect(
bb.order(ByteOrder.nativeOrder());
vertexBuffer = bb.asFloatBuffer();
vertexBuffer.put(squareCoords);
vertexBuffer.position(0);

bb = ByteBuffer.allocateDirect(texture.length * 4);
bb.order(ByteOrder.nativeOrder());
textureBuffer = bb.asFloatBuffer();
textureBuffer.put(texture);
textureBuffer.position(0);

ByteBuffer dlb = ByteBuffer.allocateDirect(
dlb.order(ByteOrder.nativeOrder());
drawListBuffer = dlb.asShortBuffer();
drawListBuffer.put(drawOrder);
drawListBuffer.position(0);
```

```
int vertexShader = SBGGameRenderer.loadShader(GLES20.GL_VERTEX_SHADER,
vertexShaderCode);
int fragmentShader = SBGGameRenderer.loadShader(GLES20.GL_FRAGMENT_SHADER,
fragmentShaderCode);

mProgram = GLES20.glCreateProgram();
GLES20.glAttachShader(mProgram, vertexShader);
GLES20.glAttachShader(mProgram, fragmentShader);
GLES20.glLinkProgram(mProgram);
}

public void draw(float[] mvpMatrix, float scroll) {
GLES20.glUseProgram(mProgram);

mPositionHandle = GLES20.glGetAttribLocation(mProgram, "vPosition");

GLES20.glEnableVertexAttribArray(mPositionHandle);

int vsTextureCoord = GLES20.glGetAttribLocation(mProgram, "TexCoordIn");
GLES20.glVertexAttribPointer(mPositionHandle, COORDS_PER_VERTEX,
GLES20.GL_FLOAT, false,
vertexStride, vertexBuffer);
GLES20.glVertexAttribPointer(vsTextureCoord, COORDS_PER_TEXTURE,
GLES20.GL_FLOAT, false,
textureStride, textureBuffer);
GLES20.glEnableVertexAttribArray(vsTextureCoord);
GLES20.glActiveTexture(GLES20.GL_TEXTURE0);
GLES20.glBindTexture(GLES20.GL_TEXTURE_2D, textures[0]);
int fsTexture = GLES20.glGetUniformLocation(mProgram, "TexCoordOut");
int fsScroll = GLES20.glGetUniformLocation(mProgram, "scroll");
GLES20.glUniform1i(fsTexture, 0);
GLES20.glUniform1f(fsScroll, scroll);
mMVPMatrixHandle = GLES20.glGetUniformLocation(mProgram, "uMVPMatrix");

GLES20.glUniformMatrix4fv(mMVPMatrixHandle, 1, false, mvpMatrix, 0);

GLES20.glDrawElements(GLES20.GL_TRIANGLES, drawOrder.length,
GLES20.GL_UNSIGNED_SHORT, drawListBuffer);

GLES20.glDisableVertexAttribArray(mPositionHandle);
}
}
```

If you are comparing this code to that in Chapter 7, you should notice one small change to the OpenGL ES 2/3 version. The scroll variable has been moved to the constructor. This allows you to pass in the amount of scroll so that you can scroll multiple instantiations of the background at different rates.

Instantiate the two new SBGBackground() in your game, as follows:

```
private SBGBackground background1 = new SBGBackground();
private SBGBackground background2 = new SBGBackground();
```

Now you need to load the images and map them as textures using the loadTexture() method of the SBGBackground(). The code for loading the textures should be called in the onSurfaceCreated() method of the Renderer.

```
public void onSurfaceCreated(GL10gl, EGLConfigconfig) {
//TODO Auto-generated method stub

...

background1.loadTexture(gl, R.drawable.starfield, context);
background1.loadTexture(gl, R.drawable.debrisfield, context);
}
```

The next two solutions will cover scrolling the background textures, now that they have been loaded.

8.2 Scroll Two Background Images

Problem

Only one of the background images scrolls.

Solution

Modify the game loop so both images scroll, by modifying the scroll variable for each image.

How It Works

The first step in the solution is to create four variables that will be used to track the current location of the background texture and the value by which to translate the texture, respectively.

```
int bgScroll1 = 0;
int bgScroll2 = 0;

float SCROLL_BACKGROUND_1 = .002f;
float SCROLL_BACKGROUND_2 = .002f;
```

These variables can be local to your Renderer class, or you can store them in a separate class. This solution takes a lot from a solution in Chapter 7. However, keeping track of multiple moving elements in your game can be tricky if you do not start off slow. Try to avoid skipping through this, as it can be easy to miss an important detail.

The onDrawFrame() method, within an implementation of an OpenGL ES Renderer, is called on every iteration of the game loop. Create a new method, called scrollBackgrounds(), that will be called from the onDrawFrame() method. See Listings 8-3 and 8-4.

Listing 8-3. scrollBackgrounds() (OpenGL ES 1)

```
private void scrollBackgrounds(GL10gl){
if (bgScroll1 == Float.MAX_VALUE){
bgScroll1 = 0f;
}

if (bgScroll2 == Float.MAX_VALUE){
bgScroll2 = 0f;
}

gl.glMatrixMode(GL10.GL_MODELVIEW);
gl.glLoadIdentity();
gl.glPushMatrix();
gl.glScalef(1f, 1f, 1f);
gl.glTranslatef(0f, 0f, 0f);

gl.glMatrixMode(GL10.GL_TEXTURE);
gl.glLoadIdentity();
gl.glTranslatef(0.0f, bgScroll1, 0.0f);

background1.draw(gl);
gl.glPopMatrix();
bgScroll1 +=  SCROLL_BACKGROUND_1;
gl.glLoadIdentity();

gl.glMatrixMode(GL10.GL_TEXTURE);
gl.glLoadIdentity();
gl.glTranslatef(0.0f, bgScroll2, 0.0f);

background2.draw(gl);
gl.glPopMatrix();
bgScroll2 +=  SCROLL_BACKGROUND_2;
gl.glLoadIdentity();

}
```

Listing 8-4. scrollBackgrounds() (OpenGL ES 2/3)

```
private void scrollBackgrounds(GL10gl){
if (bgScroll1 == Float.MAX_VALUE){
bgScroll1 = 0f;
}

if (bgScroll2 == Float.MAX_VALUE){
bgScroll2 = 0f;
}
```

```
background1.draw(mMVPMatrix, bgScroll1);
background2.draw(mMVPMatrix, bgScroll2);
bgScroll1 +=  SCROLL_BACKGROUND_1;
bgScroll2 +=  SCROLL_BACKGROUND_2;
}
```

The first part of this method tests the current value of the bgScroll1 and bgScroll2 variables. Just as in Chapter 7, the if statements are necessary to insure you do not overload your floats.

The view matrix and texture matrix models are scaled and translated to provide the needed "movement" of the background images.

Finally, call the new scrollBackgrounds() method from the onDrawFrame() method and both background images should scroll across the screen together. The background should appear as in Figure 8-3.

Figure 8-3. Both background images together

8.3 Scroll Two Background Images at Different Speeds

Problem

The background images don't scroll at different speeds.

Solution

Add a sense of depth by modifying the game loop to scroll multiple background images at different speeds.

How It Works

Building on the previous solution, only one change needs to be made to scroll the background images at different speeds.

Ideally, to create an artificial sense of depth, you would want the foreground image (of the two images) to scroll at a faster speed than the image that is furthest in the background.

To accomplish this effect, change the value of SCROLL_BACKGROUND_2 from the previous solution to a higher number. The higher the number that you set it to, the faster the image will scroll.

```
int bgScroll1 = 0;
int bgScroll2 = 0;

float SCROLL_BACKGROUND_1 = .002f;
float SCROLL_BACKGROUND_2 = .005f;
```

Chapter 9

Syncing the Background to Character Movement

In Chapter 8, solutions were presented for creating a multi-layered background that could scroll. However, you might be having problems if you tried to sync the scrolling of the background with the movement of the character.

In this chapter, you will be presented with two recipes—the first for scrolling a multi-image background in two directions, and the second for syncing the scrolling of that background with the movement of the playable character.

9.1 Scroll the Background in Two Directions

Problem

The background scrolls only in one direction when the player can run in two.

Solution

Modify the background class to track movement in two directions.

How It Works

This solution assumes that your game, possibly a platform-style game, has a character that can move in two directions. Thinking back to popular platform-style games (such as Super Mario Brothers), many times the playable character can move to the right to advance in the game. The character can also move to the left, often in a limited capacity, to retrace their steps.

Before the background can be synced with the character, it needs to be able to move in two directions. This solution will take a three-image background, load it, and scroll it to the right and then reverse it to scroll to the left.

The first step is to copy the three images that will be used as the background into the res/drawable folder. Figures 9-1 through 9-3 represent the three images that I used in this example. Notice that they are layers for a single background that have been pulled apart so that they can be scrolled at different speeds.

Figure 9-1. The farthest background layer

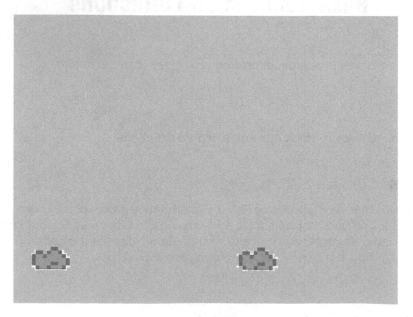

Figure 9-2. The middle-ground layer

Figure 9-3. The ground layer

> **Note**   The transparent portions of the images have been colored grey for the purpose of printing the images in thisbook.

Once the images are in the project, instantiate three instances of the SBGBackground() class—one for each layer of the background.

```
private SBGBackground background1 = new SBGBackground();
private SBGBackground background2 = new SBGBackground();
private SBGBackground background3 = new SBGBackground();
```

The next step is to create three sets of variables to control and track the speed and location of each layer of the background.

```
private float bgScroll1;
private float bgScroll2;
private float bgScroll3;
public static float SCROLL_BACKGROUND_1 = .002f;
public static float SCROLL_BACKGROUND_2 = .003f;
public static float SCROLL_BACKGROUND_3 = .004f;
```

In Chapter 7 (Listings 7-1 and 7-2), a solution was presented for creating a scrollBackground() method.

Change that method to allow the background to be scrolled either to the left or to the right, depending on which way the player is moving.

Early in the book, a solution was provided to allow a character to move across the screen (using a spritesheet). Part of this solution required the creation of a handful of variables for tracking the player's movements. Use those same variables in this solution.

```
public static int playerAction = 0;
public static final int PLAYER_MOVE_LEFT = 1;
public static final int PLAYER_MOVE_RIGHT = 2;
```

> **Note**   The aforementioned variable should be set when you collect the player's input. For more information on doing this, see Chapters 5 and 6.

Add a new parameter to the scrollBackground() method that accepts the playerAction variable, using both OpenGL ES 1 and 2/3, as shown next.

For OpenGL ES 1:

```
private void scrollBackground1(GL10gl, int direction){

...

}
```

For OpenGL ES 2/3:

```
private void scrollBackground1(int direction){

...

}
```

The direction that is passed into the scrollBackground() method will be used to determine how to scroll the background image. In the current scrollBackground() method, the following line controls the scrolling of the image:

```
bgScroll1 +=  SCROLL_BACKGROUND_1;
```

The key part of this line is the +=. To change the direction of the scroll, the operator needs to be changed from += to -=. Create a switch...case statement to make this operator change based on the direction collected from the player input.

The scrollBackground() method for OpenGL ES 1 and OpenGL ES 2/3 is shown in Listings 9-1 and 9-2, respectively.

Listing 9-1. scrollBackground() (OpenGL ES 1)

```
private void scrollBackground1(GL10gl, int direction){
if (bgScroll1 == Float.MAX_VALUE){
bgScroll1 = 0f;
}
```

```
gl.glMatrixMode(GL10.GL_MODELVIEW);
gl.glLoadIdentity();
gl.glPushMatrix();
gl.glScalef(1f, 1f, 1f);
gl.glTranslatef(0f, 0f, 0f);

gl.glMatrixMode(GL10.GL_TEXTURE);
gl.glLoadIdentity();
gl.glTranslatef(bgScroll1,0.0f, 0.0f);

background1.draw(gl);
gl.glPopMatrix();
switch(direction)
{
case PLAYER_MOVE_RIGHT:
bgScroll1 +=  SCROLL_BACKGROUND_1;
break;
case PLAYER_MOVE_LEFT:
bgScroll1 -=  SCROLL_BACKGROUND_1;
break;
}
gl.glLoadIdentity();

}
```

Listing 9-2. scrollBackground( ) (OpenGL ES 2/3)

```
private void scrollBackground1(int direction){
if (bgScroll1 == Float.MAX_VALUE){
bgScroll1 = 0f;
}

background1.draw(mMVPMatrix, bgScroll1);
switch(direction)
{
case PLAYER_MOVE_RIGHT:
bgScroll1 +=  SCROLL_BACKGROUND_1;
break;
case PLAYER_MOVE_LEFT:
bgScroll1 -=  SCROLL_BACKGROUND_1;
break;
}
}
```

The background will now scroll either to the right or to the left, based on what direction is passed into the scrollBackground( ) method. The next solution ties this method into the movement of the player.

9.2 Move the Background in Response to User Input

Problem

The background does not start or stop scrolling, based on the player movement.

Solution

The scrollBackground() method needs to be called in conjunction with the movePlayer() method to control the movement of both.

How It Works

In Chapter 6, Listing 6-7 presented a solution that created a movePlayer() method to facilitate the animation of the character. This method needs to be modified to allow the scrolling of the background to be synced to it. First, change the name of it to indicate its new purpose.

In OpenGL ES 1:

```
private void movePlayerAndBackground(GL10gl){

...

}
```

In OpenGL ES 2/3:

```
private void movePlayerAndBackground(){

...

}
```

Notice that in the existing movePlayer() method, there is a switch statement that moves the player (using a spritesheet). The switch statement needs to be rewritten so that when the character reaches roughly the middle of the screen, it does not move any further (see Listings 9-3 and 9-4). The character should appear to run in place at this point and the background should scroll to approximate movement.

Listing 9-3. movePlayerAndBackground()(OpenGL ES 1)

```
private void movePlayerAndBackground(GL10gl){
background1.draw(gl);
if(!goodguy.isDead)
{
switch(playerAction){
case PLAYER_MOVE_RIGHT:
```

```
currentStandingFrame = STANDING_RIGHT;

currentRunAniFrame += .25f;
if (currentRunAniFrame> .75f)
{
currentRunAniFrame = .0f;
}

if(playerCurrentLocation>= 3f)
{
scrollBackground1(gl, playerAction);
gl.glMatrixMode(GL10.GL_MODELVIEW);
gl.glLoadIdentity();
gl.glPushMatrix();
gl.glScalef(.15f, .15f, 1f);
gl.glTranslatef(playerCurrentLocation, .75f, 0f);
gl.glMatrixMode(GL10.GL_TEXTURE);
gl.glLoadIdentity();
gl.glTranslatef(currentRunAniFrame,.50f, 0.0f);
goodguy.draw(gl,spriteSheets,SBG_RUNNING_PTR);
gl.glPopMatrix();
gl.glLoadIdentity();

}else{
playerCurrentLocation += PLAYER_RUN_SPEED;
gl.glMatrixMode(GL10.GL_MODELVIEW);
gl.glLoadIdentity();
gl.glPushMatrix();
gl.glScalef(.15f, .15f, 1f);
gl.glTranslatef(playerCurrentLocation, .75f, 0f);
gl.glMatrixMode(GL10.GL_TEXTURE);
gl.glLoadIdentity();
gl.glTranslatef(currentRunAniFrame,.50f, 0.0f);
goodguy.draw(gl,spriteSheets,SBG_RUNNING_PTR);
gl.glPopMatrix();
gl.glLoadIdentity();

}

break;

case PLAYER_MOVE_LEFT:

currentStandingFrame = STANDING_LEFT;

currentRunAniFrame += .25f;
if (currentRunAniFrame> .75f)
{
currentRunAniFrame = .0f;
}
```

```
if(playerCurrentLocation<= 2.5f)
{
scrollBackground1(gl, playerAction);
gl.glMatrixMode(GL10.GL_MODELVIEW);
gl.glLoadIdentity();
gl.glPushMatrix();
gl.glScalef(.15f, .15f, 1f);
gl.glTranslatef(playerCurrentLocation, .75f, 0f);
gl.glMatrixMode(GL10.GL_TEXTURE);
gl.glLoadIdentity();
gl.glTranslatef(currentRunAniFrame,.75f, 0.0f);
goodguy.draw(gl,spriteSheets,SBG_RUNNING_PTR);
gl.glPopMatrix();
gl.glLoadIdentity();

}else{
playerCurrentLocation -= PLAYER_RUN_SPEED;
gl.glMatrixMode(GL10.GL_MODELVIEW);
gl.glLoadIdentity();
gl.glPushMatrix();
gl.glScalef(.15f, .15f, 1f);
gl.glTranslatef(playerCurrentLocation, .75f, 0f);
gl.glMatrixMode(GL10.GL_TEXTURE);
gl.glLoadIdentity();
gl.glTranslatef(currentRunAniFrame,.75f, 0.0f);
goodguy.draw(gl,spriteSheets,SBG_RUNNING_PTR);
gl.glPopMatrix();
gl.glLoadIdentity();

}
break;

case PLAYER_STAND:
gl.glMatrixMode(GL10.GL_MODELVIEW);
gl.glLoadIdentity();
gl.glPushMatrix();
gl.glScalef(.15f, .15f, 1f);
gl.glTranslatef(playerCurrentLocation, .75f, 0f);
gl.glMatrixMode(GL10.GL_TEXTURE);
gl.glLoadIdentity();
gl.glTranslatef(currentStandingFrame,.25f, 0.0f);
goodguy.draw(gl,spriteSheets,SBG_RUNNING_PTR);
gl.glPopMatrix();
gl.glLoadIdentity();
break;
}
}
}
```

Listing 9-4. movePlayerAndBackground()(OpenGL ES 2/3)

```
private void movePlayerAndBackground(){
background1.draw(mMVPMatrix, bgScroll1);
if(!goodguy.isDead)
{
switch(playerAction){
case PLAYER_MOVE_RIGHT:

currentStandingFrame = STANDING_RIGHT;

currentRunAniFrame += .25f;
if (currentRunAniFrame> .75f)
{
currentRunAniFrame = .0f;
}

if(playerCurrentLocation>= 3f)
{
scrollBackground1(playerAction);
goodguy.draw(spriteSheets,SBG_RUNNING_PTR, currentRunAniFrame, .75f);
}else{
playerCurrentLocation += PLAYER_RUN_SPEED;
goodguy.draw(spriteSheets,SBG_RUNNING_PTR, currentRunAniFrame, .50f);
}

break;

case PLAYER_MOVE_LEFT:
currentStandingFrame = STANDING_LEFT;

currentRunAniFrame += .25f;
if (currentRunAniFrame> .75f)
{
currentRunAniFrame = .0f;
}

if(playerCurrentLocation<= 2.5f)
{
scrollBackground1(playerAction);
goodguy.draw(spriteSheets,SBG_RUNNING_PTR, currentRunAniFrame, .75f);

}else{
playerCurrentLocation -= PLAYER_RUN_SPEED;
goodguy.draw(spriteSheets,SBG_RUNNING_PTR, currentRunAniFrame, .50f);
}
break;
```

```
case PLAYER_STAND:
goodguy.draw(spriteSheets,SBG_RUNNING_PTR, currentStandingFrame, .25f);

break;
}
}
}
```

The character animation stops progressing across the screen about midway. The method then calls the scrollBackground() method to begin moving the background.

10

Building a Level Using Tiles

In this chapter, you will be presented with two solutions for building a level out of tiles. Many 2D games (specifically, side-scrolling platform and top-down adventure/RTS-style games), implement levels that are built with repeatable tiles.

If you have had trouble building levels from tiles, this chapter should help. The first recipe will look at loading up the tiles from a sprite sheet and creating a level map. The second recipe will use the sprite sheet and the level map to then create a full level from the tiles.

10.1 Load Tiles from a Sprite Sheet
Problem

The tiles used to create a level are stored in a sprite sheet, and there is no way to determine which tile to use in which position.

Solution

Use a texture loader to map the tile texture to a set of vertices, and use a level map to dictate which tiles to place where.

How It Works

This solution requires the use of two classes. The first class holds the information for creating the vertices and indexes, and a method for drawing the tiles. The second class holds the texture information.

In Chapter 6, solutions were provided for loading sprite sheets. These solutions separated the texture loading method from the object class to allow for multiple sprite sheets to be loaded and held in one place. This solution will expand on that texture class to hold the new tile sprite sheet. As always, start by copying your sprite sheet into the project. The sprite sheet for this example, shown in Figure 10-1, has two tiles in it. One tile is a ground tile, with some grass and a bit of sky; and the second tile is a sky tile. Keep in mind, yours could have hundreds.

Figure 10-1. *A sprite sheet with two tiles*

The SBGTile() Class

With the image added to the project, create a new class, SBGTile(). The SBGTile() class will set up your vertices and indexes (see Listings 10-1 and 10-2). The structure of the class should look very familiar, as it has now been used in several other solutions; however, the bolded code has been changed to allow for the loading of multiple sprite sheets.

Listing 10-1. SBGTile()(OpenGL ES 1)

```
public class SBGTile {

private FloatBuffer vertexBuffer;
private FloatBuffer textureBuffer;
private ByteBuffer indexBuffer;

private float vertices[] = {
0.0f, 0.0f, 0.0f,
1.0f, 0.0f, 0.0f,
1.0f, 1.0f, 0.0f,
0.0f, 1.0f, 0.0f,
};

private float texture[] = {
0.0f, 0.0f,
.25f, 0f,
.25f, .25f,
0f, .25f,
};
```

```
private byte indices[] = {
0,1,2,
0,2,3,
};

public SBGTile() {
ByteBufferbyteBuf = ByteBuffer.allocateDirect(vertices.length * 4);
byteBuf.order(ByteOrder.nativeOrder());
vertexBuffer = byteBuf.asFloatBuffer();
vertexBuffer.put(vertices);
vertexBuffer.position(0);

byteBuf = ByteBuffer.allocateDirect(texture.length * 4);
byteBuf.order(ByteOrder.nativeOrder());
textureBuffer = byteBuf.asFloatBuffer();
textureBuffer.put(texture);
textureBuffer.position(0);

indexBuffer = ByteBuffer.allocateDirect(indices.length);
indexBuffer.put(indices);
indexBuffer.position(0);
}

public void draw(GL10gl,int[] spriteSheet,int currentSheet) {
gl.glBindTexture(GL10.GL_TEXTURE_2D, spriteSheet[currentSheet - 1]);

gl.glFrontFace(GL10.GL_CCW);
gl.glEnable(GL10.GL_CULL_FACE);
gl.glCullFace(GL10.GL_BACK);

gl.glEnableClientState(GL10.GL_VERTEX_ARRAY);
gl.glEnableClientState(GL10.GL_TEXTURE_COORD_ARRAY);

gl.glVertexPointer(3, GL10.GL_FLOAT, 0, vertexBuffer);
gl.glTexCoordPointer(2, GL10.GL_FLOAT, 0, textureBuffer);

gl.glDrawElements(GL10.GL_TRIANGLES, indices.length, GL10.GL_UNSIGNED_BYTE, indexBuffer);

gl.glDisableClientState(GL10.GL_VERTEX_ARRAY);
gl.glDisableClientState(GL10.GL_TEXTURE_COORD_ARRAY);
gl.glDisable(GL10.GL_CULL_FACE);
}

}
```

Listing 10-2. SBGTile() (OpenGL ES 2/3)

```
class SBGBackground{
private final String vertexShaderCode =
"uniform mat4 uMVPMatrix;" +
"attribute vec4 vPosition;" +
"attribute vec2 TexCoordIn;" +
```

```java
"varying vec2 TexCoordOut;" +
"void main() {" +
"  gl_Position = uMVPMatrix * vPosition;" +
"  TexCoordOut = TexCoordIn;" +
"}";
private final String fragmentShaderCode =
"precision mediump float;" +
"uniform vec4 vColor;" +
"uniform sampler2D TexCoordIn;" +
"uniform float posX;" +
"uniform float posY;" +
"varying vec2 TexCoordOut;" +
"void main() {" +
" gl_FragColor = texture2D(TexCoordIn, vec2(TexCoordOut.x+
posX,TexCoordOut.y + posY));"+
"}";
private float texture[] = {
0f, 0f,
.25f, 0f,
.25f, .25f,
0f, .25f,
};

private int[] textures = new int[1];
private final FloatBuffer vertexBuffer;
private final ShortBuffer drawListBuffer;
private final FloatBuffer textureBuffer;
private final int mProgram;
private int mPositionHandle;
private int mMVPMatrixHandle;

static final int COORDS_PER_VERTEX = 3;
static final int COORDS_PER_TEXTURE = 2;
static float squareCoords[] = { -1f,  1f, 0.0f,
-1f, -1f, 0.0f,
1f, -1f, 0.0f,
1f,  1f, 0.0f };

private final short drawOrder[] = { 0, 1, 2, 0, 2, 3 };

private final int vertexStride = COORDS_PER_VERTEX * 4;
public static int textureStride = COORDS_PER_TEXTURE * 4;

public SBGBackground() {
ByteBuffer bb = ByteBuffer.allocateDirect(

bb.order(ByteOrder.nativeOrder());
vertexBuffer = bb.asFloatBuffer();
vertexBuffer.put(squareCoords);
vertexBuffer.position(0);
```

```java
bb = ByteBuffer.allocateDirect(texture.length * 4);
bb.order(ByteOrder.nativeOrder());
textureBuffer = bb.asFloatBuffer();
textureBuffer.put(texture);
textureBuffer.position(0);

ByteBuffer dlb = ByteBuffer.allocateDirect(
dlb.order(ByteOrder.nativeOrder());
drawListBuffer = dlb.asShortBuffer();
drawListBuffer.put(drawOrder);
drawListBuffer.position(0);

int vertexShader = SBGGameRenderer.loadShader(
GLES20.GL_VERTEX_SHADER,vertexShaderCode);
int fragmentShader = SBGGameRenderer.loadShader(
GLES20.GL_FRAGMENT_SHADER,fragmentShaderCode);

mProgram = GLES20.glCreateProgram();
GLES20.glAttachShader(mProgram, vertexShader);
GLES20.glAttachShader(mProgram, fragmentShader);
GLES20.glLinkProgram(mProgram);
}

public void draw(float[] mvpMatrix, float posX, float posY,
int[] spriteSheet, int currentSheet)    {
GLES20.glUseProgram(mProgram);
GLES20.glBindTexture(GLES20.GL_TEXTURE_2D, spriteSheet[currentSheet - 1]);
mPositionHandle = GLES20.glGetAttribLocation(mProgram, "vPosition");
GLES20.glEnableVertexAttribArray(mPositionHandle);
int vsTextureCoord = GLES20.glGetAttribLocation(mProgram, "TexCoordIn");
GLES20.glVertexAttribPointer(mPositionHandle, COORDS_PER_VERTEX,
GLES20.GL_FLOAT, false,
vertexStride, vertexBuffer);
GLES20.glVertexAttribPointer(vsTextureCoord, COORDS_PER_TEXTURE,
GLES20.GL_FLOAT, false,
textureStride, textureBuffer);
GLES20.glEnableVertexAttribArray(vsTextureCoord);
GLES20.glActiveTexture(GLES20.GL_TEXTURE0);
int fsTexture = GLES20.glGetUniformLocation(mProgram, "TexCoordOut");
int fsPosX = GLES20.glGetUniformLocation(mProgram, "posX");
int fsPosY = GLES20.glGetUniformLocation(mProgram, "posY");
GLES20.glUniform1i(fsTexture, 0);
GLES20.glUniform1f(fsPosX, posX);
GLES20.glUniform1f(fsPosY, posY);
mMVPMatrixHandle = GLES20.glGetUniformLocation(mProgram, "uMVPMatrix");

GLES20.glUniformMatrix4fv(mMVPMatrixHandle, 1, false, mvpMatrix, 0);

GLES20.glDrawElements(GLES20.GL_TRIANGLES, drawOrder.length,
GLES20.GL_UNSIGNED_SHORT, drawListBuffer);

GLES20.glDisableVertexAttribArray(mPositionHandle);
}
}
```

Pay particular attention to the bolded lines. These lines take in an int array representing the multiple sprite sheet textures, and an int that indicates which sprite sheet to use for the specific draw operation.

The SBGTextures() Class

Now you need a class to handle the loading of the multiple sprite sheets. Create a new class named SBGTextures(), as shown in Listings 10-3 and 10-4.

Listing 10-3. SBGTextures()(OpenGL ES 1)

```
public class SBGTextures {

private int[] textures = new int[2];

public SBGTextures(GL10gl){

gl.glGenTextures(2, textures, 0);

}
public int[] loadTexture(GL10gl,int texture, Context context,int textureNumber) {
InputStream imagestream = context.getResources().openRawResource(texture);
Bitmap bitmap = null;
Bitmap temp = null;

Matrix flip = new Matrix();
flip.postScale(-1f, -1f);

try {

temp = BitmapFactory.decodeStream(imagestream);
bitmap = Bitmap.createBitmap(temp, 0, 0, temp.getWidth(), temp.getHeight(), flip, true);
}catch(Exception e){

}finally {
//Always clear and close
try {
imagestream.close();
imagestream = null;
} catch (IOException e) {
}
}

gl.glBindTexture(GL10.GL_TEXTURE_2D, textures[textureNumber - 1]);

gl.glTexParameterf(GL10.GL_TEXTURE_2D, GL10.GL_TEXTURE_MIN_FILTER, GL10.GL_NEAREST);
gl.glTexParameterf(GL10.GL_TEXTURE_2D, GL10.GL_TEXTURE_MAG_FILTER, GL10.GL_LINEAR);

gl.glTexParameterf(GL10.GL_TEXTURE_2D, GL10.GL_TEXTURE_WRAP_S, GL10.GL_CLAMP_TO_EDGE);
gl.glTexParameterf(GL10.GL_TEXTURE_2D, GL10.GL_TEXTURE_WRAP_T, GL10.GL_CLAMP_TO_EDGE);
```

```
GLUtils.texImage2D(GL10.GL_TEXTURE_2D, 0, bitmap, 0);

bitmap.recycle();

return textures;
}
}
```

Listing 10-4. SBGTextures() (OpenGL ES 2/3)

```
public class SBGTextures {

private int[] textures = new int[2];

public SBGTextures(){
}

public void loadTexture(int texture, Context context, int textureNumber) {
InputStream imagestream = context.getResources().openRawResource(texture);
Bitmap bitmap = null;

android.graphics.Matrix flip = new android.graphics.Matrix();
flip.postScale(-1f, -1f);

try {

bitmap = BitmapFactory.decodeStream(imagestream);

}catch(Exception e){
//Handle your exceptions here
}finally {
try {
imagestream.close();
imagestream = null;
} catch (IOException e) {
//Handle your exceptions here
}
}

GLES20.glGenTextures(2, textures, 0);
GLES20.glBindTexture(GLES20.GL_TEXTURE_2D, textures[textureNumber - 1]);

GLES20.glTexParameterf(GLES20.GL_TEXTURE_2D, GLES20.GL_TEXTURE_MIN_FILTER, GLES20.GL_NEAREST);
GLES20.glTexParameterf(GLES20.GL_TEXTURE_2D, GLES20.GL_TEXTURE_MAG_FILTER, GLES20.GL_LINEAR);

GLES20.glTexParameterf(GLES20.GL_TEXTURE_2D, GLES20.GL_TEXTURE_WRAP_S, GLES20.GL_REPEAT);
GLES20.glTexParameterf(GLES20.GL_TEXTURE_2D, GLES20.GL_TEXTURE_WRAP_T, GLES20.GL_REPEAT);

GLUtils.texImage2D(GLES20.GL_TEXTURE_2D, 0, bitmap, 0);

bitmap.recycle();
}
}
```

Again, pay attention to the bolded line in each listing. The int array used here means that you can expand the number of separate sprite sheets that you can hold, as you need to.

Instantiate the required classes, and create a sprite sheet array, in your Renderer.

```
private SBGTile tiles = new SBGTile();
private SBGTextures textureloader;
private int[] spriteSheets = new int[2];
```

Then, in the onSurfaceCreated() method of the Renderer, set the textureloader, and use it to load the tiles sprite sheet.

```
textureloader = new SBGTextures(gl);
spriteSheets = textureloader.loadTexture(gl, R.drawable.tiles, context, 1);
```

Now the tiles (as a texture) are ready to use. But how does the game know where to put the tiles? For this, you need to create a level map.

Create a Level Map

A level map is a representation of where the game should place each tile. The map will be a two-dimensional array of ints.

The map is built like a matrix of int values. Each int value represents a specific tile. The example in this solution has only two different tiles; therefore, the level map would be made of only 0s and 1s. The 0s would represent the ground tile, and the 1s would represent the sky tiles.

Creating these level maps as two-dimensional arrays is a quick and easy way for storing the architecture of many levels. Here is an example of the two-dimensional array level map for this solution.

```
int map[][] = {
{0,0,0,0,0,0,0,0,0,0},
{1,1,1,1,1,1,1,1,1,1},
{1,1,1,1,1,1,1,1,1,1},
{1,1,1,1,1,1,1,1,1,1},
{1,1,1,1,1,1,1,1,1,1},
{1,1,1,1,1,1,1,1,1,1},
{1,1,1,1,1,1,1,1,1,1},
{1,1,1,1,1,1,1,1,1,1},
{1,1,1,1,1,1,1,1,1,1},
{1,1,1,1,1,1,1,1,1,1},
};
```

Here we have created a 10x10array of 0s and 1s to represent where the tiles should be placed on the screen. In the next solution, you will write a tiles engine that will read this array and actually place the tiles on the screen in the correct places.

10.2 Create a Level from Tiles

Problem

Your game cannot read the level map int array to create a level using tiles.

Solution

Create a tile engine that reads in the array and writes out tiles in the desired locations.

How It Works

This solution takes you through building a tile engine. A tile engine reads in a level map array, one dimension at a time, and then draws tiles based on the value in the array.

In the previous solution, we created an array of only two values, 0 and 1. These values correspond to the two tiles in the sprite sheet. Keep in mind that you could easily have many more tiles, giving you a much more elaborate-looking level.

> **Tip** If you use more tiles, and thus have more ints in your array, the only change you will have to make to this tile engine is to add more cases to the switch...case statement.

The first step is to create a drawTiles() method in your Renderer.

For OpenGL ES 1:

```
private void drawtiles(GL10 gl, int[][] map){

}
```

For OpenGL ES 2/3:

```
private void drawtiles(int[][] map){

}
```

The drawTiles() method will take in your two-dimensional array map and loop through it. However, before you can loop through the array, you need to set up two variables.

The purpose of these variables will be to translate the model matrix when you are setting the tiles in place. The concept here is that you read in the first element of the map array, then set and draw the corresponding tile. Then you have to translate the model matrix to the next position on the screen in order to place the next tile.

```
float tileLocY = 0f;
float tileLocX = 0f;
```

Now, create a nested for loop that will iterate the two dimensions of the map array.

```
for(int x=0; x<10; x++){
for(int y=0; y<10; y++){

}
}
```

The first order of business, if you are using OpenGL ES 1, is to scale and translate the model matrix, then set up the texture matrix.

```
for(int x=0; x<10; x++){
for(int y=0; y<10; y++){

gl.glMatrixMode(GL10.GL_MODELVIEW);
gl.glLoadIdentity();
gl.glPushMatrix();
gl.glScalef(.20f, .20f, 1f);
gl.glTranslatef(tileLocY, tileLocX, 0f);

gl.glMatrixMode(GL10.GL_TEXTURE);
gl.glLoadIdentity();
}
}
```

Notice in the bolded code that the model matrix is being translated by the tileLocY and tileLocX values that were set earlier. As the loop progress, these variables will be incremented so that the next tile will be placed in the correct location.

The next step is to set up a simple switch...case statement to read the current element of the map array.

```
for(int x=0; x<10; x++){
for(int y=0; y<10; y++){

gl.glMatrixMode(GL10.GL_MODELVIEW);
gl.glLoadIdentity();
gl.glPushMatrix();
gl.glScalef(.20f, .20f, 1f);
gl.glTranslatef(tileLocY, tileLocX, 0f);

gl.glMatrixMode(GL10.GL_TEXTURE);
gl.glLoadIdentity();

switch(map[x][y]){
case 1:
break;
case 0:
break;
}
}
}
```

Because, at this point, the matrix mode is already set to texture, the only thing you have to do in the switch...case statement is translate the sprite sheet to the correct tile image.

```
switch(map[x][y]){
case 1:
gl.glTranslatef(.75f,.75f, 0f);
break;
case 0:
gl.glTranslatef(.75f,1f, 0f);
break;
}
```

> **Tip**   For more information about working with sprite sheets, see Chapter 6, "Loading a Sprite Sheet."

The tile is in place, and the texture is set to the correct image. Now draw the tile and increment the tileLocY variable to move to the next position.

```
switch(map[x][y]){
case 1:
gl.glTranslatef(.75f,.75f, 0f);
break;
case 0:
gl.glTranslatef(.75f,1f, 0f);
break;
}
tiles.draw(gl, spriteSheets, SBG_TILE_PTR);
tileLocY += .50;
```

The remainder of the nested loops pop the matrix on each new row, and the advance the tileLocX variable as needed.

If you are using OpenGL ES 2/3, the concept remains the same, but the process is slightly different. You still need to loop through each value of the map, and use a switch statement to act upon each case. The difference is that rather than translate the matrix, as in OpenGL ES 1, you can simply pass the location of each tile to the drawtiles() method. This is the same process that you use to work with a sprite sheet (see Chapter 6 for a more in-depth discussion of sprite sheets). Listing 10-5 shows what the completed method should look like. The completed OpenGL ES 2/3 version of drawtiles() is shown in Listing 10-6.

Listing 10-5. drawtiles() (OpenGL ES 1)

```
private void drawtiles(GL10gl){
float tileLocY = 0f;
float tileLocX = 0f;
for(int x=0; x<10; x++){
for(int y=0; y<10; y++){
```

```
gl.glMatrixMode(GL10.GL_MODELVIEW);
gl.glLoadIdentity();
gl.glPushMatrix();
gl.glScalef(.20f, .20f, 1f);
gl.glTranslatef(tileLocY, tileLocX, 0f);

gl.glMatrixMode(GL10.GL_TEXTURE);
gl.glLoadIdentity();

switch(map[x][y]){
case 1:
gl.glTranslatef(.75f,.75f, 0f);
break;
case 0:
gl.glTranslatef(.75f,1f, 0f);
break;
}
tiles.draw(gl, spriteSheets, SBG_TILE_PTR);
tileLocY += .50;
}
gl.glPopMatrix();
gl.glLoadIdentity();
tileLocY = 0f;
tileLocX += .50;
}
}
```

Listing 10-6. drawtiles()(OpenGL ES 2/3)

```
private void drawtiles(){
float tileLocY = 0f;
float tileLocX = 0f;
Matrix.translateM(mTMatrix, 0, tileLocX, tileLocT, 0);
Matrix.multiplyMM(mMVPMatrix, 0, mTMatrix, 0, mMVPMatrix, 0) ;
for(int x=0; x<10; x++){
for(int y=0; y<10; y++){

switch(map[x][y]){
case 1:
tiles.draw(mMPVMatrix, .75f, .75, spriteSheets, SBG_TILE_PTR);
break;
case 0:
tiles.draw(mMPVMatrix, .75f, .75, spriteSheets, SBG_TILE_PTR);
break;
}

tileLocY += .50;
}
tileLocY = 0f;
tileLocX += .50;
}
}
```

If you are using OpenGL ES 2/3, be sure to set up a new translation matrix (mTMatrix in Listing 10-6) in your Renderer. The job of the translation matrix is to move the location of the tile. It is the OpenGL ES 2/3 equivalent of glTranslatef(). The code that follows shows the translation matrix.

```
public class SBGGameRenderer implements GLSurfaceView.Renderer {
...
private final float[] mTMatrix = new float[16];
...
@Override
public void onDrawFrame(GL10 unused) {
GLES20.glClear(GLES20.GL_COLOR_BUFFER_BIT);
Matrix.setLookAtM(mVMatrix, 0, 0, 0, -3, 0f, 0f, 0f, 0f, 1.0f, 0.0f);
Matrix.multiplyMM(mMVPMatrix, 0, mProjMatrix, 0, mVMatrix, 0);
drawtiles();


...


}
}
```

The level produced by this map array and sprite sheet combination is shown in Figure 10-2.

Figure 10-2. A simple level built with a level map and tiles

Remember, to utilize more tiles, simply expand the scope of your switch...case statement.

11

Moving a Character

Moving a character around the screen—whether it's a person, animal, robot, or vehicle—is one of the more crucial parts of a compelling game. Chances are, if you have tried to create a character that moves freely in a game, you have run into some problems.

This chapter will present solutions to help you move your character around. Solutions in this chapter include making a character run, and changing the character animation when the character is moving.

The first solution helps you move your character in four directions on the screen. The remaining solutions help you move your character at different speeds and animate your character as it moves.

11.1 Move a Character in Four Directions

Problem

The character on the screen will not move.

Solution

Use the game loop to control the movement of the character.

How It Works

This solution requires you to track where the player wants the character to move, then translate that intent to the x or y axis of the model matrix. In other words, once you have captured where the player wants to move, you can use a switch...case statement to determine which axis to translate in the model matrix, thus moving the character on the screen accordingly.

You complete this solution in three steps. You need to determine which direction the player wants to move in, then create a flag that holds this value, and finally use that value to move the character on the screen. The first step is to capture which direction the player wants to move. We will accomplish this by using the SimpleOnGestureListener().

The player will swipe left, right, up, or down to indicate which direction the character should run (think something similar to a Temple Run–style input system).In the game's main intent, instantiate a new SimpleOnGestureListener(), as shown in Listing 11-1.

Listing 11-1. SimpleOnGestureListener()

```
GestureDetector.SimpleOnGestureListener gestureListener =
new GestureDetector.SimpleOnGestureListener(){
@Override
public boolean onDown(MotionEventarg0) {
//TODO Auto-generated method stub
return false;
}

@Override
public boolean onFling(MotionEvente1, MotionEvente2, float velocityX,
float velocityY) {

float leftMotion = e1.getX() - e2.getX();
float upMotion = e1.getY() - e2.getY();

float rightMotion = e2.getX() - e1.getX();
float downMotion = e2.getY() - e1.getY();

if((leftMotion == Math.max(leftMotion, rightMotion)) &&
(leftMotion>Math.max(downMotion, upMotion)) )
{
}

if((rightMotion == Math.max(leftMotion, rightMotion)) &&
(rightMotion>Math.max(downMotion, upMotion) )
{
}
if((upMotion == Math.max(upMotion, downMotion)) &&
(upMotion>Math.max(leftMotion, rightMotion)) )
{
}

if((downMotion == Math.max(upMotion, downMotion)) &&
(downMotion>Math.max(leftMotion, rightMotion)) )
{
}
return false;
}
```

```
@Override
public void onLongPress(MotionEvent e) {
//TODO Auto-generated method stub

}
@Override
public boolean onScroll(MotionEvente1, MotionEvente2, float distanceX,
float distanceY) {
//TODO Auto-generated method stub
return false;
}
@Override
public void onShowPress(MotionEvent e) {
//TODO Auto-generated method stub

}
@Override
public boolean onSingleTapUp(MotionEvent e) {
//TODO Auto-generated method stub
return false;
}

};
```

Notice the four if statements within this instantiation. They represent the left, right, up, and down actions. Now create an int that can be accessed from both the main intent and the game loop. Set the int according to which direction the SimpleOnGestureListener() has detected (see Listing 11-2).

Listing 11-2. SimpleOnGestureListener()

```
public static int playeraction = 0;
public static final int PLAYER_MOVE_LEFT = 1;
public static final int PLAYER_MOVE_RIGHT = 2;
public static final int PLAYER_MOVE_UP = 3;
public static final int PLAYER_MOVE_DOWN = 4;

...

if((leftMotion == Math.max(leftMotion, rightMotion)) &&
(leftMotion>Math.max(downMotion, upMotion)) )
{
playeraction = PLAYER_MOVE_LEFT;
}

if((rightMotion == Math.max(leftMotion, rightMotion)) &&
(rightMotion>Math.max(downMotion, upMotion) )
{
playeraction = PLAYER_MOVE_RIGHT;
}
```

```
if((upMotion == Math.max(upMotion, downMotion)) &&
(upMotion>Math.max(leftMotion, rightMotion)) )
{
playeraction = PLAYER_MOVE_UP;
}

if((downMotion == Math.max(upMotion, downMotion)) &&
(downMotion>Math.max(leftMotion, rightMotion)) )
{
playeraction = PLAYER_MOVE_DOWN;
}
```

...

Finally, in the Renderer, create a method that reads the value of the int you just set and translates the model matrix of the character accordingly, as shown in Listings 11-3 and 11-4.

Listing 11-3. movePlayer()(OpenGL ES 1)

```
private void movePlayer(GL10gl){
switch(playeraction){
case PLAYER_MOVE_RIGHT:

gl.glMatrixMode(GL10.GL_MODELVIEW);
gl.glLoadIdentity();
gl.glPushMatrix();
gl.glTranslatef(0f, .75f, 0f);
character.draw(gl);
gl.glPopMatrix();
gl.glLoadIdentity();

break;
case PLAYER_MOVE_LEFT:

gl.glMatrixMode(GL10.GL_MODELVIEW);
gl.glLoadIdentity();
gl.glPushMatrix();
gl.glTranslatef(0f, -.75f, 0f);
character.draw(gl);
gl.glPopMatrix();
gl.glLoadIdentity();
break;

case PLAYER_MOVE_UP:

gl.glMatrixMode(GL10.GL_MODELVIEW);
gl.glLoadIdentity();
gl.glPushMatrix();
gl.glTranslatef(.75f, 0f, 0f);
character.draw(gl);
```

```
gl.glPopMatrix();
gl.glLoadIdentity();

break;
case PLAYER_MOVE_DOWN:

gl.glMatrixMode(GL10.GL_MODELVIEW);
gl.glLoadIdentity();
gl.glPushMatrix();
gl.glTranslatef(-.75f, 0f, 0f);
character.draw(gl);
gl.glPopMatrix();
gl.glLoadIdentity();
break;

}
}
```

Listing 11-4. movePlayer()(OpenGL ES 2/3)

```
private void movePlayer(GL10gl){
switch(playeraction){
case PLAYER_MOVE_RIGHT:

Matrix.translateM(mTMatrix, 0, 0, .75f, 0);
Matrix.multiplyMM(mMVPMatrix, 0, mTMatrix, 0, mMVPMatrix, 0)
character.draw(mMVPMatrix);

break;
case PLAYER_MOVE_LEFT:

Matrix.translateM(mTMatrix, 0, 0, -.75f, 0);
Matrix.multiplyMM(mMVPMatrix, 0, mTMatrix, 0, mMVPMatrix, 0)
character.draw(mMVPMatrix);
break;

case PLAYER_MOVE_UP:

Matrix.translateM(mTMatrix, 0, .75f, 0, 0);
Matrix.multiplyMM(mMVPMatrix, 0, mTMatrix, 0, mMVPMatrix, 0)
character.draw(mMVPMatrix);
break;
case PLAYER_MOVE_DOWN:

Matrix.translateM(mTMatrix, 0, -.75f, 0, 0);
Matrix.multiplyMM(mMVPMatrix, 0, mTMatrix, 0, mMVPMatrix, 0)
character.draw(mMVPMatrix);
break;

}
}
```

The calls to glTranslatef() have been highlighted in bold in Listing 11-3 (for the OpenGL ES 1code) because you should translate your model matrix by whatever values work best in your specific game.

11.2 Move a Character at Different Speeds

Problem

The game character needs to walk and run at different speeds.

Solution

Use a count of game loops to determine when the character should change speeds.

How It Works

In this solution, you count the number of game loops that have been executed and use this count to determine when the character's speed should change. For example, your game is built in such a way that the character will move right when the player touches the right side of the screen, the character will move left when the player touches the left side of the screen, and the character stands still when the player is not touching the screen. You can use this architecture to let the character walk if the player just touches the screen for a short amount of time, and then run if the player touches the screen longer.

Tip   Chapter 5 outlines solutions for setting up a game with touch-based controls.

The first step is to create two variables that are scoped to be read from any class in your game. The first variable is to track the number of game loops that have been executed, and the second variable tracks the current speed of the character.

```
public static final float PLAYER_RUN_SPEED = .15f;
public static int totalGameLoops = 0;
```

Next, create a movePlayer() method in the Renderer class. This method has been used in multiple solutions thus far in this book. If you need a base explanation of how this method works, please see Chapter 6.

The movePlayer() method contains a switch...case statement that reads the actions of the player and moves the character accordingly. Modify this method to test for the number of executed loops and change the speed of the character based on this (see Listings 11-5 and 11-6).

Listing 11-5. Varying the Speed of Movement (OpenGL ES 1)

```
private void movePlayer(GL10gl){
if (totalGameLoops> 15)
{
PLAYER_RUN_SPEED += .5f;
}

switch(playeraction){
case PLAYER_MOVE_RIGHT:

playercurrentlocation += PLAYER_RUN_SPEED;
gl.glMatrixMode(GL10.GL_MODELVIEW);
gl.glLoadIdentity();
gl.glPushMatrix();
gl.glTranslatef(playercurrentlocation, 0f, 0f);
goodguy.draw(gl);
gl.glPopMatrix();
gl.glLoadIdentity();

break;
case PLAYER_MOVE_LEFT:

playercurrentlocation -= PLAYER_RUN_SPEED;
gl.glMatrixMode(GL10.GL_MODELVIEW);
gl.glLoadIdentity();
gl.glPushMatrix();
gl.glTranslatef(playercurrentlocation, 0f, 0f);
goodguy.draw(gl);
gl.glPopMatrix();
gl.glLoadIdentity();

break;

case PLAYER_STAND:

PLAYER_RUN_SPEED = .15f;
totalGameLoops = 0;

break;
}
}
```

Listing 11-6. Varying the Speed of Movement (OpenGL ES 2/3)

```
private void movePlayer(GL10gl){
if (totalGameLoops> 15)
{
PLAYER_RUN_SPEED += .5f;
}
```

```
switch(playeraction){
case PLAYER_MOVE_RIGHT:
playercurrentlocation += PLAYER_RUN_SPEED;
Matrix.translateM(mTMatrix, 0, 0, playercurrentlocation, 0);
Matrix.multiplyMM(mMVPMatrix, 0, mTMatrix, 0, mMVPMatrix, 0)
character.draw(mMVPMatrix);

break;
case PLAYER_MOVE_LEFT:
playercurrentlocation -= PLAYER_RUN_SPEED;
Matrix.translateM(mTMatrix, 0, 0, playercurrentlocation, 0);
Matrix.multiplyMM(mMVPMatrix, 0, mTMatrix, 0, mMVPMatrix, 0)
character.draw(mMVPMatrix);
break;

case PLAYER_STAND:

PLAYER_RUN_SPEED = .15f;
totalGameLoops = 0;

break;
}

}
```

Finally, in the onDrawFrame() method of the Renderer, increment the totalGameLoops int with each execution (see Listing 11-7).

Listing 11-7. totalGameLoops

```
public void onDrawFrame(GL10gl) {

...

totalGameLoops +=1;
movePlayer(gl);

...
}
```

11.3 Animate a Character When It Moves
Problem

The game character does not appear to be walking when it moves.

Solution

Use spritesheet animation to make the character appear to walk when it moves.

How It Works

This solution will involve making a modification to the movePlayer() method that you have been working with quite extensively. After the model matrix is translated, translate the texture matrix to present the next frame in the spritesheet.

Note   For solutions on working with spritesheets, see Chapter 6.

First create a scoped variable, visible from all classes, that will be used to track the current frame of spritesheet animation.

```
public static float currentrunaniframe = 0f;
```

Next, make the bolded changes to the movePlayer() method (see Listings 11-8 and 11-9).

Listing 11-8. Animating the Character (OpenGL ES 1)

```
private void movePlayer(GL10gl){
if (totalGameLoops> 15)
{
PLAYER_RUN_SPEED += .5f;
}

currentrunaniframe += .25f;
if (currentrunaniframe> .75f)
{
currentrunaniframe = .0f;
}


switch(playeraction){
case PLAYER_MOVE_RIGHT:

playercurrentlocation += PLAYER_RUN_SPEED;
scrollBackground1(gl, playeraction);
gl.glMatrixMode(GL10.GL_MODELVIEW);
gl.glLoadIdentity();
gl.glPushMatrix();
gl.glTranslatef(playercurrentlocation, 0f, 0f);
gl.glMatrixMode(GL10.GL_TEXTURE);
gl.glLoadIdentity();
gl.glTranslatef(currentrunaniframe,.50f, 0.0f);
goodguy.draw(gl);
gl.glPopMatrix();
gl.glLoadIdentity();

break;
```

```
case PLAYER_MOVE_LEFT:

playercurrentlocation -= PLAYER_RUN_SPEED;
scrollBackground1(gl, playeraction);
gl.glMatrixMode(GL10.GL_MODELVIEW);
gl.glLoadIdentity();
gl.glPushMatrix();
gl.glTranslatef(playercurrentlocation, 0f, 0f);
gl.glMatrixMode(GL10.GL_TEXTURE);
gl.glLoadIdentity();
gl.glTranslatef(currentrunaniframe,.75f, 0.0f);
goodguy.draw(gl);
gl.glPopMatrix();
gl.glLoadIdentity();

break;

case PLAYER_STAND:

PLAYER_RUN_SPEED = .15f;
totalGameLoops = 0;

break;
}
}
```

Listing 11-9. Animating the Character (OpenGL ES 2/3)

```
private void movePlayer(GL10gl){
if (totalGameLoops> 15)
{
PLAYER_RUN_SPEED += .5f;
}
currentrunaniframe += .25f;
if (currentrunaniframe> .75f)
{
currentrunaniframe = .0f;
}

switch(playeraction){
case PLAYER_MOVE_RIGHT:
playercurrentlocation += PLAYER_RUN_SPEED;
Matrix.translateM(mTMatrix, 0, 0, playercurrentlocation, 0);
Matrix.multiplyMM(mMVPMatrix, 0, mTMatrix, 0, mMVPMatrix, 0)
character.draw(mMVPMatrix,currentrunaniframe, .50f );

break;
case PLAYER_MOVE_LEFT:
```

```
playercurrentlocation -= PLAYER_RUN_SPEED;
Matrix.translateM(mTMatrix, 0, 0, playercurrentlocation, 0);
Matrix.multiplyMM(mMVPMatrix, 0, mTMatrix, 0, mMVPMatrix, 0)
character.draw(mMVPMatrix,currentrunaniframe, .75f );
break;

case PLAYER_STAND:

PLAYER_RUN_SPEED = .15f;
totalGameLoops = 0;

break;
}


}
```

The bolded if statement in Listing 11-8 works based on four frames of animation. If there are four frames of character animation in the sprite sheet, after four loops the animation needs to be reset to the first frame. The if statement tests the current frame, and resets the animation if it has reached the fourth frame.

The key to animating the character (if you are working in OpenGL ES 2/3) is to modify the draw() method of your character class to pass in the x and y locations of the sprite sheet image that you want to display (see Chapter 6 for a detailed solution to accomplish this).

Finally, modify the PLAYER_STAND case to change the animation from to a static "standing" image. Keep in mind that depending on the setup of your spritesheet, the coordinates presented in this solution might need to be altered (see Listings 11-10 and 11-11).

Listing 11-10. PLAYER_STAND (OpenGL ES 1)

```
case PLAYER_STAND:

PLAYER_RUN_SPEED = .15f;
totalGameLoops = 0;
gl.glMatrixMode(GL10.GL_MODELVIEW);
gl.glLoadIdentity();
gl.glPushMatrix();
gl.glTranslatef(playercurrentlocation, 0f, 0f);
gl.glMatrixMode(GL10.GL_TEXTURE);
gl.glLoadIdentity();
gl.glTranslatef(.25f,.25f, 0.0f);
goodguy.draw(gl);
gl.glPopMatrix();
gl.glLoadIdentity();

break;
```

Listing 11-11. PLAYER_STAND (OpenGL ES 2/3)

```
case PLAYER_STAND:

PLAYER_RUN_SPEED = .15f;
totalGameLoops = 0;
playercurrentlocation -= PLAYER_RUN_SPEED;
Matrix.translateM(mTMatrix, 0, 0, playercurrentlocation, 0);
Matrix.multiplyMM(mMVPMatrix, 0, mTMatrix, 0, mMVPMatrix, 0)
character.draw(mMVPMatrix,.25f, .25f );

break;
```

Moving an Enemy

Moving a character around the screen—be it a person, animal, robot, or vehicle—is one of the more crucial parts of a compelling game. Chances are, if you have tried to create a character that moves freely in a game, you have run into some issue.

This chapter will present solutions to help you add enemies to your game. Solutions in this chapter include loading enemies into predetermined locations within your game, and moving enemies along a specific path.

12.1 Load Enemies to Predetermined Locations

Problem

The game does not load enemies in the correct locations.

Solution

Use a class to determine where enemy spawn points are.

How It Works

Many game types have "spawn points" where characters will generate. To spawn enemies in these predetermined locations, you need to add some floats to your enemy class and then use these floats to translate the model matrix of the enemy to the spawn location.

The solutions in this chapter will be based on a basic character class, which in turn is based on the SBGBackground class from Chapters 7 and 8. Given that we are talking about enemies within the game now, let's rename the class SBGEnemy. The contents of the class should appear as shown in Listings 12-1 and 12-2.

Listing 12-1. SBGEnemy() (OpenGL ES 1)

```
public class SBGEnemy {

private FloatBuffer vertexBuffer;
private FloatBuffer textureBuffer;
private ByteBuffer indexBuffer;

private float vertices[] = {
0.0f, 0.0f, 0.0f,
1.0f, 0.0f, 0.0f,
1.0f, 1.0f, 0.0f,
0.0f, 1.0f, 0.0f,
};

private float texture[] = {
0.0f, 0.0f,
0.25f, 0.0f,
0.25f, 0.25f,
0.0f, 0.25f,
};

private byte indices[] = {
0,1,2,
0,2,3,
};

public SBGEnemy() {

ByteBuffer byteBuf = ByteBuffer.allocateDirect(vertices.length * 4);
byteBuf.order(ByteOrder.nativeOrder());
vertexBuffer = byteBuf.asFloatBuffer();
vertexBuffer.put(vertices);
vertexBuffer.position(0);

byteBuf = ByteBuffer.allocateDirect(texture.length * 4);
byteBuf.order(ByteOrder.nativeOrder());
textureBuffer = byteBuf.asFloatBuffer();
textureBuffer.put(texture);
textureBuffer.position(0);

indexBuffer = ByteBuffer.allocateDirect(indices.length);
indexBuffer.put(indices);
indexBuffer.position(0);
}

public void draw(GL10gl, int[] spriteSheet) {
gl.glBindTexture(GL10.GL_TEXTURE_2D, spriteSheet[0]);
gl.glFrontFace(GL10.GL_CCW);
gl.glEnable(GL10.GL_CULL_FACE);
gl.glCullFace(GL10.GL_BACK);
```

```
gl.glEnableClientState(GL10.GL_VERTEX_ARRAY);
gl.glEnableClientState(GL10.GL_TEXTURE_COORD_ARRAY);

gl.glVertexPointer(3, GL10.GL_FLOAT, 0, vertexBuffer);
gl.glTexCoordPointer(2, GL10.GL_FLOAT, 0, textureBuffer);

gl.glDrawElements(GL10.GL_TRIANGLES, indices.length, GL10.GL_UNSIGNED_BYTE, indexBuffer);

gl.glDisableClientState(GL10.GL_VERTEX_ARRAY);
gl.glDisableClientState(GL10.GL_TEXTURE_COORD_ARRAY);
gl.glDisable(GL10.GL_CULL_FACE);
    }

}
```

Listing 12-2. SBGEnemy() (OpenGL ES 2/3)

```
public class SBGEnemy {

private final String vertexShaderCode =
"uniform mat4 uMVPMatrix;" +

"attribute vec4 vPosition;" +
"attribute vec2 TexCoordIn;" +
"varying vec2 TexCoordOut;" +
"void main() {" +
"  gl_Position = uMVPMatrix * vPosition;" +
"  TexCoordOut = TexCoordIn;" +
"}";

private final String fragmentShaderCode =
"precision mediump float;" +
"uniform vec4 vColor;" +
"uniform sampler2D TexCoordIn;" +
"uniform float texX;" +
"uniform float texY;" +
"varying vec2 TexCoordOut;" +
"void main() {" +
" gl_FragColor = texture2D(TexCoordIn, vec2(TexCoordOut.x +
texX,TexCoordOut.y + texY));"+
"}";
private float texture[] = {
0f, 0f,
.25f, 0f,
.25f, .25f,
0f, .25f,
};

private int[] textures = new int[1];
private final FloatBuffer vertexBuffer;
private final ShortBuffer indexBuffer;
private final FloatBuffer textureBuffer;
```

```java
private final int mProgram;
private int mPositionHandle;
private int mMVPMatrixHandle;

static final int COORDS_PER_VERTEX = 3;
static final int COORDS_PER_TEXTURE = 2;
static float vertices[] = { -1f,  1f, 0.0f,
-1f, -1f, 0.0f,
1f, -1f, 0.0f,
1f,  1f, 0.0f };

private final short indices[] = { 0, 1, 2, 0, 2, 3 };

private final int vertexStride = COORDS_PER_VERTEX * 4;
public static int textureStride = COORDS_PER_TEXTURE * 4;

public SBGEnemy() {

ByteBuffer byteBuf = ByteBuffer.allocateDirect(vertices.length * 4);
byteBuf.order(ByteOrder.nativeOrder());
vertexBuffer = byteBuf.asFloatBuffer();
vertexBuffer.put(vertices);
vertexBuffer.position(0);

byteBuf = ByteBuffer.allocateDirect(texture.length * 4);
byteBuf.order(ByteOrder.nativeOrder());
textureBuffer = byteBuf.asFloatBuffer();
textureBuffer.put(texture);
textureBuffer.position(0);

indexBuffer = ByteBuffer.allocateDirect(indices.length);
indexBuffer.put(indices);
indexBuffer.position(0);

int vertexShader = SBGGameRenderer.loadShader(
GLES20.GL_VERTEX_SHADER, vertexShaderCode);
int fragmentShader = SBGGameRenderer.loadShader(
GLES20.GL_FRAGMENT_SHADER,fragmentShaderCode);

mProgram = GLES20.glCreateProgram();
GLES20.glAttachShader(mProgram, vertexShader);
GLES20.glAttachShader(mProgram, fragmentShader);
GLES20.glLinkProgram(mProgram);
}

public void draw(float[] mvpMatrix, int texX, int texY, int[] spriteSheet) {
GLES20.glUseProgram(mProgram);

mPositionHandle = GLES20.glGetAttribLocation(mProgram, "vPosition");

GLES20.glEnableVertexAttribArray(mPositionHandle);
```

```
int vsTextureCoord = GLES20.glGetAttribLocation(mProgram, "TexCoordIn");
GLES20.glVertexAttribPointer(mPositionHandle, COORDS_PER_VERTEX,
GLES20.GL_FLOAT, false,
vertexStride, vertexBuffer);
GLES20.glVertexAttribPointer(vsTextureCoord, COORDS_PER_TEXTURE,
GLES20.GL_FLOAT, false,
textureStride, textureBuffer);
GLES20.glEnableVertexAttribArray(vsTextureCoord);
GLES20.glActiveTexture(GLES20.GL_TEXTURE0);
GLES20.glBindTexture(GLES20.GL_TEXTURE_2D, spriteSheet[0]);

int fsTexture = GLES20.glGetUniformLocation(mProgram, "TexCoordOut");
int fsTexX = GLES20.glGetUniformLocation(mProgram, "texX");
int fsTexY = GLES20.glGetUniformLocation(mProgram, "texY");
GLES20.glUniform1i(fsTexture, 0);
GLES20.glUniform1f(fsTexX, texX);
GLES20.glUniform1f(fsTexY, texY);

mMVPMatrixHandle = GLES20.glGetUniformLocation(mProgram, "uMVPMatrix");

GLES20.glUniformMatrix4fv(mMVPMatrixHandle, 1, false, mvpMatrix, 0);

GLES20.glDrawElements(GLES20.GL_TRIANGLES, drawOrder.length,
GLES20.GL_UNSIGNED_SHORT, indexBuffer);

GLES20.glDisableVertexAttribArray(mPositionHandle);
    }
}
```

Then modify this class and add two floats. One float will track the x axis spawn location and the other float will track the y axis spawn location (see Listing 12-3).

Listing 12-3. Floats for Tracking Spawn Location

```
public class SBGEnemy {

public float posY = 0f;
public float posX = 0f;

...

}
```

Set these floats to the desired spawn location in the SBGEnemy constructor (see Listing 12-4).

Listing 12-4. Assigning Values to the Location Floats

```
public class SBGEnemy {

public float posY = 0f;
public float posX = 0f;
...
```

```
public SBGEnemy() {
posX = .25;
posY = .25;
...
}
...

}
```

Now you can use the SBGEnemy.posX and SBGEnemy.posY in the glTranslatef() method call for OpenGL ES 1 to move the model matrix of the enemy to the spawn location before you draw it. You can use the same properties in the Matrix.translateM() method for OpenGL ES 2/3. The spawnEnemy() method, shown in Listings 12-5 and 12-6, can be created in your game to help you spawn enemies in a location.

Listing 12-5. spawnEnemy()(OpenGL ES 1)

```
private SFEnemy enemy = new SFEnemy();

spawnEnemy(){
gl.glMatrixMode(GL10.GL_MODELVIEW);
gl.glLoadIdentity();
gl.glPushMatrix();
gl.glScalef(.25f, .25f, 1f);
gl.glTranslatef(enemy.posX, enemy.posY, 0f);
}
```

Listing 12-6. spawnEnemy()(OpenGL ES 2/3)

```
private SFEnemy enemy = new SFEnemy();

spawnEnemy(){
Matrix.translateM(mTMatrix, 0, enemy.posX, enemy.posY, 0);
Matrix.multiplyMM(mMVPMatrix, 0, mTMatrix, 0, mMVPMatrix, 0);
}
```

12.2 Load Enemies to Random Locations

Problem

The game needs to spawn enemies in random locations.

Solution

Modify the last solution to create "random" locations for spawning enemies.

How It Works

Many games will spawn enemies in random locations. This adds a level of difficulty to your game by taking away the predictability of predetermined spawn locations.

The code from the last solution can easily be modified to generate random spawn locations. Listings 12-7 and 12-8 show the modification that should be made to accommodate having a random spawn location.

Listing 12-7. SBGEnemy( ) for Random Locations (OpenGL ES 1)

```java
public class SBGEnemy {

public float posY = 0f;
public float posX = 0f;

private FloatBuffer vertexBuffer;
private FloatBuffer textureBuffer;
private ByteBuffer indexBuffer;

private float vertices[] = {
0.0f, 0.0f, 0.0f,
1.0f, 0.0f, 0.0f,
1.0f, 1.0f, 0.0f,
0.0f, 1.0f, 0.0f,
};

private float texture[] = {
0.0f, 0.0f,
0.25f, 0.0f,
0.25f, 0.25f,
0.0f, 0.25f,
};

private byte indices[] = {
0,1,2,
0,2,3,
};

public SBGEnemy() {
Random randomPos = new Random();
posX = randomPos.nextFloat() * 3;
posY = randomPos.nextFloat() * 3;

ByteBuffer byteBuf = ByteBuffer.allocateDirect(vertices.length * 4);
byteBuf.order(ByteOrder.nativeOrder());
vertexBuffer = byteBuf.asFloatBuffer();
vertexBuffer.put(vertices);
vertexBuffer.position(0);
```

```java
byteBuf = ByteBuffer.allocateDirect(texture.length * 4);
byteBuf.order(ByteOrder.nativeOrder());
textureBuffer = byteBuf.asFloatBuffer();
textureBuffer.put(texture);
textureBuffer.position(0);

indexBuffer = ByteBuffer.allocateDirect(indices.length);
indexBuffer.put(indices);
indexBuffer.position(0);
}

public void draw(GL10gl, int[] spriteSheet) {
gl.glBindTexture(GL10.GL_TEXTURE_2D, spriteSheet[0]);

gl.glFrontFace(GL10.GL_CCW);
gl.glEnable(GL10.GL_CULL_FACE);
gl.glCullFace(GL10.GL_BACK);

gl.glEnableClientState(GL10.GL_VERTEX_ARRAY);
gl.glEnableClientState(GL10.GL_TEXTURE_COORD_ARRAY);

gl.glVertexPointer(3, GL10.GL_FLOAT, 0, vertexBuffer);
gl.glTexCoordPointer(2, GL10.GL_FLOAT, 0, textureBuffer);

gl.glDrawElements(GL10.GL_TRIANGLES, indices.length, GL10.GL_UNSIGNED_BYTE, indexBuffer);

gl.glDisableClientState(GL10.GL_VERTEX_ARRAY);
gl.glDisableClientState(GL10.GL_TEXTURE_COORD_ARRAY);
gl.glDisable(GL10.GL_CULL_FACE);
    }

}
```

Listing 12-8. SBGEnemy( ) for Random Locations (OpenGL ES 2/3)

```java
public class SBGEnemy {

private final String vertexShaderCode =
"uniform mat4 uMVPMatrix;" +

"attribute vec4 vPosition;" +
"attribute vec2 TexCoordIn;" +
"varying vec2 TexCoordOut;" +
"void main() {" +
"  gl_Position = uMVPMatrix * vPosition;" +
"  TexCoordOut = TexCoordIn;" +
"}";

private final String fragmentShaderCode =
"precision mediump float;" +
"uniform vec4 vColor;" +
"uniform sampler2D TexCoordIn;" +
```

```
"uniform float texX;" +
"uniform float texY;" +
"varying vec2 TexCoordOut;" +
"void main() {" +
" gl_FragColor = texture2D(TexCoordIn, vec2(TexCoordOut.x +
texX,TexCoordOut.y + texY));"+
"}";
private float texture[] = {
0f, 0f,
.25f, 0f,
.25f, .25f,
0f, .25f,
};

private int[] textures = new int[1];
private final FloatBuffer vertexBuffer;
private final ShortBuffer indexBuffer;
private final FloatBuffer textureBuffer;
private final int mProgram;
private int mPositionHandle;
private int mMVPMatrixHandle;

static final int COORDS_PER_VERTEX = 3;
static final int COORDS_PER_TEXTURE = 2;
static float vertices[] = { -1f,  1f, 0.0f,
-1f, -1f, 0.0f,
1f, -1f, 0.0f,
1f,  1f, 0.0f };

private final short indices[] = { 0, 1, 2, 0, 2, 3 };

private final int vertexStride = COORDS_PER_VERTEX * 4;
public static int textureStride = COORDS_PER_TEXTURE * 4;

public SBGEnemy() {
Random randomPos = new Random();
posX = randomPos.nextFloat() * 3;
posY = randomPos.nextFloat() * 3;

ByteBuffer byteBuf = ByteBuffer.allocateDirect(vertices.length * 4);
byteBuf.order(ByteOrder.nativeOrder());
vertexBuffer = byteBuf.asFloatBuffer();
vertexBuffer.put(vertices);
vertexBuffer.position(0);

byteBuf = ByteBuffer.allocateDirect(texture.length * 4);
byteBuf.order(ByteOrder.nativeOrder());
textureBuffer = byteBuf.asFloatBuffer();
textureBuffer.put(texture);
textureBuffer.position(0);
```

```
indexBuffer = ByteBuffer.allocateDirect(indices.length);
indexBuffer.put(indices);
indexBuffer.position(0);

int vertexShader = SBGGameRenderer.loadShader(
GLES20.GL_VERTEX_SHADER,vertexShaderCode);
int fragmentShader = SBGGameRenderer.loadShader(
GLES20.GL_FRAGMENT_SHADER,fragmentShaderCode);

mProgram = GLES20.glCreateProgram();
GLES20.glAttachShader(mProgram, vertexShader);
GLES20.glAttachShader(mProgram, fragmentShader);
GLES20.glLinkProgram(mProgram);
}

public void draw(float[] mvpMatrix, int texX, int texY, int[] spriteSheet) {
GLES20.glUseProgram(mProgram);

mPositionHandle = GLES20.glGetAttribLocation(mProgram, "vPosition");

GLES20.glEnableVertexAttribArray(mPositionHandle);

int vsTextureCoord = GLES20.glGetAttribLocation(mProgram, "TexCoordIn");
GLES20.glVertexAttribPointer(mPositionHandle, COORDS_PER_VERTEX,
GLES20.GL_FLOAT, false,
vertexStride, vertexBuffer);
GLES20.glVertexAttribPointer(vsTextureCoord, COORDS_PER_TEXTURE,
GLES20.GL_FLOAT, false,
textureStride, textureBuffer);
GLES20.glEnableVertexAttribArray(vsTextureCoord);
GLES20.glActiveTexture(GLES20.GL_TEXTURE0);
GLES20.glBindTexture(GLES20.GL_TEXTURE_2D, spriteSheet[0]);

int fsTexture = GLES20.glGetUniformLocation(mProgram, "TexCoordOut");
int fsTexX = GLES20.glGetUniformLocation(mProgram, "texX");
int fsTexY = GLES20.glGetUniformLocation(mProgram, "texY");
GLES20.glUniform1i(fsTexture, 0);
GLES20.glUniform1f(fsTexX, texX);
GLES20.glUniform1f(fsTexY, texY);

mMVPMatrixHandle = GLES20.glGetUniformLocation(mProgram, "uMVPMatrix");

GLES20.glUniformMatrix4fv(mMVPMatrixHandle, 1, false, mvpMatrix, 0);

GLES20.glDrawElements(GLES20.GL_TRIANGLES, drawOrder.length,
GLES20.GL_UNSIGNED_SHORT, indexBuffer);

GLES20.glDisableVertexAttribArray(mPositionHandle);
    }
}
```

This solution builds on the posX and posY properties that you created in the previous solution. Rather than populate these properties with static values, the constructor of the SBGEnemy class will now populate random locations into the posX and posY floats. The result is that now when you call SBGEnemy.posX and SBGEnemy.posY from the spanEnemy() method, the enemy will be created at a random location on the screen.

12.3 Move Enemies Along a Path

Problem

The enemies do not move along a predetermined path.

Solution

Use an algorithm to create paths for the characters to automatically move along.

How It Works

This solution is geared toward moving your enemy along a specific path, known as a Bezier curve. Bezier curves are commonly used in games because they can be easily produced by a fairly simple algorithm. They can also be modified to create variations that make games interesting and unpredictable. Figure 12-1 illustrates what a Bezier curve looks like.

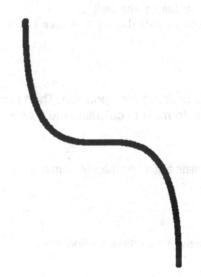

Figure 12-1. A quadratic Bezier curve

For the enemy to move in a quadratic Bezier curve from the top to the bottom of the screen, you will need two methods. You can create one method to get the next x-axis value on the Bezier curve, and one method to give you the next y-axis value on the Bezier curve. Each time you call these methods, you will be given the next place on the x and y axes that the particular enemy needs to be moved to. Once you have these locations, you use glTranslatef() to move the model matrix to the calculated position.

Luckily, it is fairly simple to plot points on a Bezier curve. To construct a quadratic Bezier curve, you need four Cartesian points: a start, an end, and two curving points somewhere in between for the curve to wrap around. Let's review how to do this now.

Create eight new floats to track the x and y coordinates of these points, as shown in Listing 12-9.

Listing 12-9. Bezier Tracking Coordinates

```
public static final float BEZIER_X_1 = 0f;
public static final float BEZIER_X_2 = 1f;
public static final float BEZIER_X_3 = 2.5f;
public static final float BEZIER_X_4 = 3f;
public static final float BEZIER_Y_1 = 0f;
public static final float BEZIER_Y_2 = 2.4f;
public static final float BEZIER_Y_3 = 1.5f;
public static final float BEZIER_Y_4 = 2.6f;
```

Modify the SBGEnemy class to add a posT float to the existing posX and posY, as shown in Listing 12-10.

Listing 12-10. posT

```
public class SBGEnemy {
public float posY = 0f; //the x position of the enemy
public float posX = 0f; //the y position of the enemy
public float posT = 0f; //the t used in calculating a Bezier curve

...
}
```

The key value in plotting the points is called the t position. The t position tells the formula where on the curve you are, thus allowing the formula to calculate the x or y coordinate for that single position.

> **Tip** If you do not understand the math behind the following formulas, there are many great resources, including a wiki, for Bezier curves.

Create two methods in your SBGEnemy() class(see Listing 12-11). One method is used to get the next x-axis value, and one is used to get the next y-axis value. Also, add random values to the posX and posY floats, and a set value to posT.

Listing 12-11. Seeding the Position Values

```
public class SBGEnemy {
public float posY = 0f; //the x position of the enemy
public float posX = 0f; //the y position of the enemy
public float posT = 0f; //the t used in calculating a Bezier curve
```

```
public SBGEnemy() {
posY = (randomPos.nextFloat() * 4) + 4;
posX = randomPos.nextFloat() * 3;
posT = .012;

}

public float getNextPosX(){

}
public float getNextPosY(){

}

}
```

The formula to find a point on a quadratic Bezier curve on the y axis is as follows:

(y1*(t3)) + (y2 * 3 * (t2) * (1-t)) + (y3 * 3 * t * (1-t)2) + (y4* (1-t)3)

Note   To get the x-axis point, simply replace y with x in the preceding equation.

Use this formula in your getNextPosY() to calculate your enemy's position (see Listing 12-12).

Listing 12-12. getNextPosY()

```
public class SBGEnemy {
public float posY = 0f; //the x position of the enemy
public float posX = 0f; //the y position of the enemy
public float posT = 0f; //the t used in calculating a Bezier curve

public SBGEnemy() {
posY = (randomPos.nextFloat() * 4) + 4;
posX = randomPos.nextFloat() * 3;
posT = .012;

}

public float getNextPosX(){

}

public float getNextPosY(){
return (float)((BEZIER_Y_1*(posT*posT*posT)) +
(BEZIER_Y_2 * 3 * (posT * posT) * (1-posT)) +
(BEZIER_Y_3 * 3 * posT * ((1-posT) * (1-posT))) +
(BEZIER_Y_4 * ((1-posT) * (1-posT) * (1-posT))));
}

}
```

Use this same formula for the x axis, with one minor change, as shown in Listing 12-13.

Listing 12-13. getNextPosX()

```
public class SBGEnemy {
public float posY = 0f; //the x position of the enemy
public float posX = 0f; //the y position of the enemy
public float posT = 0f; //the t used in calculating a Bezier curve

public SBGEnemy() {
posY = (randomPos.nextFloat() * 4) + 4;
posX = randomPos.nextFloat() * 3;
posT = sfengine.SCOUT_SPEED;

}

public float getNextPosX(){
return (float)((BEZIER_X_4*(posT*posT*posT)) +
(BEZIER_X_3 * 3 * (posT * posT) * (1-posT)) +
(BEZIER_X_2 * 3 * posT * ((1-posT) * (1-posT))) +
(BEZIER_X_1 * ((1-posT) * (1-posT) * (1-posT))));

 }

public float getNextPosY(){
return (float)((BEZIER_Y_1*(posT*posT*posT)) +
(BEZIER_Y_2 * 3 * (posT * posT) * (1-posT)) +
(BEZIER_Y_3 * 3 * posT * ((1-posT) * (1-posT))) +
(BEZIER_Y_4 * ((1-posT) * (1-posT) * (1-posT))));
}

}
```

Notice that when calculating for the right-hand side of the x axis, the values are x1, x2, x3, then x4; however, from the left-hand side, the points are used in the opposite order, x4, x3, x2, then x1.

Now, on each execution of the game loop, set the SBGEnemy.posX to SBGEnemy.getNextPosX() and set SBGEnemy.posY to SBGEnemy.getNextPosY(), and then translate the model matrix to the posX and posY points, as you have been doing.

Chapter 13

Moving a Character with Obstacles

If games, especially platform games, featured flat levels where the character simply ran from left to right unencumbered, they would not hold a player's interest for very long.

Platform games such as Super Mario Brothers, LittleBigPlanet2, and countless others contain obstacles that the player must navigate around. Using obstacles in your games is a great way to add excitement and also brake up action. However, obstacles can also be an added level of complication when it comes to coding your game.

This chapter will cover a number of scenarios where you might have had problems working with obstacles in your games. The first scenario covers letting a character jump between platforms.

13.1 Jump Between Platforms

Problem

The game does not allow the player to jump between platforms on a game level.

Solution

Use a predetermined distance, and a mathematic formula to adjust the jumping animation.

How It Works

Everyone knows what a person looks like when they jump. There is a specific motion and smoothness to a jump that can be hard to replicate in a game. In this solution, we are going to modify some of the code from earlier solutions to create a jumping action for the playable character.

The first step is to create a control for the user to "jump." In Solution 5.4, I showed you how to create a gesture using the onFling() method of the SimpleOnGestureListener. Modify that code to set a common variable for indicating that the player wants to jump.

```
GestureDetector.SimpleOnGestureListener gestureListener = new
GestureDetector.SimpleOnGestureListener(){

@Override
publicbooleanonFling(MotionEvente1, MotionEvente2, float velocityX,
floatvelocityY) {

playeraction = PLAYER_JUMPING;
}
};
```

The playeraction and PLAYER_JUMPING variables are integers that are stored in a class that is accessible to the project.

The character we are going to make jump is the SuperBanditGuy. Earlier in this book, you created a SuperBanditGuy class that created the main character for the game and moved him around the screen. Modify the SuperBanditGuy class to add two floats (x and y) that will be used to track the x and y coordinates of the character as they progress through the jump.

```
public class SuperBanditGuy {

public float x = .75f;
public float y = .75f;
//I like to start characters a little higher than the bottom of the screen so
//that the player can see some ground under them
...

}
```

Now, add the following floats to the game loop,Renderer.

```
private float previousJumpPos = 0;
private float posJump = 0;
```

Again, in a previous solution, we created a case statement in the game loop that allows you to test the playeraction and move the character accordingly. Let's now modify that case statement to test for PLAYER_JUMPING and then launch into the math for calculating the jump. Listings 13-1 and 13-2 (OpenGL ES 1 and OpenGL ES 2/3, respectively) will let your character perform a basic jump.

Listing 13-1. PLAYER_JUMPING (OpenGL ES 1)

```
switch(playeraction){
case PLAYER_MOVE_RIGHT:

...

break;
case PLAYER_JUMPING:
previousJumpPos = posJump;

posJump += (float)(((Math.PI / 2) / .5) * PLAYER_RUN_SPEED);
if (posJump<= Math.PI)
{
goodguy.y += 1.5 / .5 * .15 * PLAYER_RUN_SPEED;

}else{
goodguy.y -=(Math.sin((double)posJump) - Math.sin((double)previousJumpPos))* 1.5;
if (goodguy.y<= .75f){
playeraction = PLAYER_STAND;
goodguy.y = .75f;
}
}
goodguy.x += PLAYER_RUN_SPEED;

gl.glMatrixMode(GL10.GL_MODELVIEW);
gl.glLoadIdentity();
gl.glPushMatrix();
gl.glScalef(.15f, .15f, 1f);
gl.glTranslatef(goodguy.x, goodguy.y, 0f);
gl.glPopMatrix();
gl.glLoadIdentity();

break;
...
}
```

Listing 13-2. PLAYER_JUMPING (OpenGL ES 2/3)

```
switch(playeraction){
case PLAYER_MOVE_RIGHT:

...

break;
case PLAYER_JUMPING:
previousJumpPos = posJump;

posJump += (float)(((Math.PI / 2) / .5) * PLAYER_RUN_SPEED);
if (posJump<= Math.PI)
{
goodguy.y += 1.5 / .5 * .15 * PLAYER_RUN_SPEED;
```

```
}else{
goodguy.y -=(Math.sin((double)posJump) - Math.sin((double)previousJumpPos))* 1.5;
if (goodguy.y<= .75f){
playeraction = PLAYER_STAND;
goodguy.y = .75f;
}
}
goodguy.x += PLAYER_RUN_SPEED;

Matrix.translateM(RotationMatrix, 0, goodguy.x, goodguy.y, 0);

break;

...
}
```

The key to moving the character in a convincing jumping motion, regardless of the OpenGL ES version, is the following formula:

```
posJump += (float)(((Math.PI / 2) / .5) * PLAYER_RUN_SPEED);
if (posJump<= Math.PI)
{
goodguy.y += 1.5 / .5 * .15 * PLAYER_RUN_SPEED;
}else{
goodguy.y -=(Math.sin((double)posJump) - Math.sin((double)previousJumpPos))* 1.5;
if (goodguy.y<= .75f){
playeraction = PLAYER_STAND;
goodguy.y = .75f;
}
}
```

> **Note**   There are a number of values in this formula that you need to tweak, based on your specific game. These values include the height and the length, in time, of the jump.

Notice that this formula only acts on the y axis of the character's position. The x-axis position is going to continue to move left or right at the determined run speed of the character. Let's examine each line of this formula.

```
previousJumpPos = posJump;
```

This first line sets the previousJumpPos for use later in the formula.

```
posJump += (float)(((Math.PI / 2) / .5) * PLAYER_RUN_SPEED);
```

This line plots the position of the jump on a sine wave. This is not used to directly determine where on the screen the character is in the jump. Rather, it is used to determine, in memory, when the character has reached the peak on the jump.

The value of .5 is the length of time of the jump. While it doesn't represent a specific unit of time, it can be increased or decreased to create longer or shorter lasting jumps. The Math.PI/2, or half PI, part of the line simply represents the fact that we are starting on a plane that is already halfway into the sine wave.

When you are dealing with sine waves, PI is the amount of time it takes to cycle the wave. Therefore, the timing of our wave is half PI to PI. While the current position on the sine wave is less than PI, we know the character is in the process of going up to the apex of the jump. Once the character's position is greater than PI, we can begin to bring it back down to the ground. The purpose of the next line, the if statement, is to test for this condition.

```
if (posJump<= Math.PI)
{
goodguy.y += 1.5 / .5 * .15 * PLAYER_RUN_SPEED;
}else{
goodguy.y -=(Math.sin((double)posJump) - Math.sin((double)previousJumpPos))* 1.5;
...
}
```

Finally, within the if statement, the first condition moves the character up on the y axis, and the second condition moves it down.

```
goodguy.y += 1.5 / .5 * .15 * PLAYER_RUN_SPEED;
```

Notice that the character's y-axis position is being increased by the formula. This will move the character up on the y axis. At the same time, the character's x-axis position is being increased, as if the character were moving normally on the x axis in the direction of the jump.

The following line moves the character down.

```
goodguy.y -=(Math.sin((double)posJump) - Math.sin((double)previousJumpPos))* 1.5;
```

This formula decreases the value of the y-axis position to move the character back down to the ground level.

Note   The value of 1.5 in both of the moving statements represents the height of the jump. Again, you can adjust this value as needed for higher or shorter jumps.

When the jump is over, simply test that the character's position is once again .75 on the y axis (the starting position as defined in the float added to the renderer) and exit from the jump, as follows.

```
if (goodguy.y<= .75f){
playeraction = PLAYER_STAND;
goodguy.y = .75f;
}
```

The best placement for this code is in the `if` statement where the y-axis position is being decreased. If you place this code outside of the `if` statement, you run the risk of letting the character fall below the ground level for a split second.

Finally, draw out the character, as shown in Listings 13-3 and 13-4.

Listing 13-3. Draw the Character (OpenGL ES 1)

```
gl.glMatrixMode(GL10.GL_MODELVIEW);
gl.glLoadIdentity();
gl.glPushMatrix();
gl.glScalef(.15f, .15f, 1f);
gl.glTranslatef(goodguy.x, goodguy.y, 0f);
gl.glMatrixMode(GL10.GL_TEXTURE);
gl.glLoadIdentity();
```

Listing 13-4. Draw the Character (OpenGL ES 2/3)

```
Matrix.translateM(RotationMatrix, 0, goodguy.x, goodguy.y, 0);
```

This code can be easily added to your renderer to produce a jumping motion.

13.2 Move up Steps

Problem

The character needs to jump up or down steps, or other objects that are on uneven planes.

Solution

Use a modified version of the jumping solution to navigate steps.

How It Works

In Chapter 15, I will be presenting solutions for collision detection. While the solution in this chapter does broach the subject of collision detection, it is not as in depth as the solutions that will be presented later. Rather, this solution will specifically handle the modification of the jumping code from the last solution that will be needed to navigate steps.

If you are jumping up steps, you will start with the same code from Listings 13-1 and 13-2.

The modification that needs to be made is in the `if` statement that tests whether the character has descended far enough through the jump to reach the ground again. Replace the test value with the height of the step.

```
if (goodguy.y<= <height of step>){
playeraction = PLAYER_STAND;
goodguy.y = <height of step>;
}
```

By testing whether the character has descended to the height of the step, you can stop the movement of the character on the step. This solution requires that you either know, or test for, the height of the step.

This solution is good for levels where you can, in code, anticipate the layout of the level. For example, if you built your level using tiles, you can test the tile map to know where the step are and therefore know the height at which to stop the descent. This solution is not as good if the layout of the level can change dynamically.

If you have a level that contains debris or perhaps moving platforms and you cannot use this method, refer to Chapter 15, which has much more on collision detection.

Chapter 14

Firing Weapons

Many games require the player to fire or throw weapons at obstacles or enemies. If you have ever tried to fire weapons, you have likely encountered problems in getting your projectiles to leave your character in a predictable manner, and travel along a set path to a target.

Weapons can come in many shapes, sizes, and functions. Bullets, in many gaming situations, travel in straight lines, as do missiles, lasers, and most other propelled weapons. Thrown weapons, such as rocks, grenades, and even arrows to an extent, follow trajectories that are more parabolic. Regardless of the image or animation that you choose to use for the weapon, the math for getting it from point A to point B will be mostly the same.

This chapter will present multiple solutions for both wiring up "buttons" that will trigger weapons, and for animating the weapons on the screen. Much like Chapter 13, this chapter is not as heavy in OpenGL ES as some of the past chapters. There is more periphery coding involved when you need a character that uses weapons.

The first recipe that we will look at will offer a way to wire up a "fire button" on the screen. This button will be based on previous solutions and will give you a way to control the firing of weapons in your game.

There are multiple game scenarios where you might not need a fire button. Rather, the weapons may either fire automatically or they may even fire constantly. Weapons that fire constantly are quite popular in games such as top/down shooters. If you are planning to use a game type where the weapons fire automatically, feel free to skip the first recipe in this chapter.

14.1 Wire a "Fire" Button

Problem

The player has no way to fire weapons. A button—or interactive area of the screen—is needed to let the player fire the character's weapons.

Solution

Createan interactive space on the screen where the player can tap to trigger the firing of the weapons. This will be demonstrated in two different solutions.

How It Works

I am going to tackle this solution two ways. The first is based on a previous solution in Recipe 5.3 where the screen area was divided into touch zones. We will now dedicate one of these zones to firing. If the player touches this area of the screen, the flag for firing the weapons will be set.

This method is good for some situations; however, if the game type calls for multiple touch areas on the screen, it could lead to weapons unintentionally being fired. Therefore, a second solution will also be explored where the player can double tap anywhere on the screen to fire the weapons.

Solution 1

For the first solution, override the onTouchEvent() of the game's activity. Keep in mind that this might not necessarily be the main activity, especially if your game begins with a menu.Set the PLAYER_FIRE_WEAPONS flag when a touch is detected by this event, as shown in Listing 14-1.

Listing 14-1. onTouchEvent()

```
@Override
public boolean onTouchEvent(MotionEvent event) {
float x = event.getX();
float y = event.getY();
DisplayMetrics outMetrics = new DisplayMetrics();

display.getMetrics(outMetrics);

int height = outMetrics.heightPixels / 4;

int playableArea = outMetrics.heightPixels - height;
if (y >playableArea){
switch (event.getAction()){
case MotionEvent.ACTION_DOWN:
if(x <outMetrics.widthPixels / 2){
playeraction = PLAYER_FIRE_WEAPONS;
}
break;
}
}

return false;
}
```

In many of the solutions contained in this book, you have been working with the playeraction int. This int was established earlier in the book to act as a holder for the current action. The game loop contains a case statement that will read this int and execute the weapon firing code when playeraction = PLAYER_FIRE_WEAPONS.

> **Note** The display variable used in this solution is set in the main activity of the game. This is the activity that is started when the player launches the game. Thus, the display variable is set as follows:
>
> ```
> display = ((WindowManager)
> getSystemService(Context.WINDOW_SERVICE)).getDefaultDisplay();
> ```

If this solution is not exactly what you need, you can easily set up a different solution where the player can double tap anywhere on the screen to trigger the firing of the weapons. We will look at this solution next.

Solution 2

To detect a double tap, you need to implement the GestureDetector. The code in Listing 14-2 will allow the player to double tap on the screen and fire the weapons.

Listing 14-2. Activity with GestureDetector

```
public class SBGGameMain extends Activity {
private GestureDetector gd;

@Override
public void onCreate(Bundle savedInstanceState) {

...

gd = new GestureDetector(this,gestureListener);
}
@Override
protected void onResume() {
super.onResume();
gameView.onResume();
}

@Override
protected void onPause() {
super.onPause();
gameView.onPause();
}

@Override
public boolean onTouchEvent(MotionEvent event) {
float x = event.getX();
float y = event.getY();
DisplayMetrics outMetrics = new DisplayMetrics();
```

```
display.getMetrics(outMetrics);

int height = outMetrics.heightPixels/4;

int playableArea = outMetrics.heightPixels - height;
if (y >playableArea){
switch (event.getAction()){
case MotionEvent.ACTION_DOWN:
if(x <outMetrics.widthPixels/2){
playeraction = PLAYER_MOVE_LEFT;
}else{
playeraction = PLAYER_MOVE_RIGHT;
}
break;
case MotionEvent.ACTION_UP:
playeraction = PLAYER_STAND;
break;
}
}
else {
return gd.onTouchEvent(event);
}

return false;
}

GestureDetector.SimpleOnGestureListener gestureListener = new
GestureDetector.SimpleOnGestureListener(){
@Override
public boolean onDown(MotionEvent arg0) {
//TODO Auto-generated method stub
return false;
}

@Override
public boolean onFling(MotionEvent e1, MotionEvent e2, float velocityX,
float velocityY) {

return false;
}
@Override
public void onLongPress(MotionEvent e) {
//TODO Auto-generated method stub

}
@Override
public boolean onScroll(MotionEvent e1, MotionEvent e2, float distanceX,
float distanceY) {
//TODO Auto-generated method stub
return false;
}
```

```
@Override
public void onShowPress(MotionEvent e) {
//TODO Auto-generated method stub

}
@Override
public boolean onSingleTapUp(MotionEvent e) {
//TODO Auto-generated method stub
return false;
}
@Override
public boolean onDoubleTap(MotionEvent e) {

playeraction = PLAYER_FIRE_WEAPONS;

return false;

};

};
}
```

The key to Solution 2 is to create a GestureDetector in your activity. Then establish a new SimpleOnGestureListener() and pass the event from the onTouchEvent() to it. The SimpleOnGestureListener() will then determine if the event is the result of a double tap and set the playeraction to PLAYER_FIRE_WEAPONS.

14.2 Animate a Missile

Problem

When the player fires the weapons, a projectile should leave from the character and travel in a straight line until it hits a target or moves off the screen.

Solution

Create a new missile class and use OpenGL ES to move it from the character to the target.

How It Works

The first step is to create a new class for your weapon. This class, like many of those created in other solutions in this book, will draw the square for your image's texture, and then map your texture into the square. The new class for drawing the weapon should look like that shown in Listings 14-3 (OpenGL ES 1) and 14-4 (OpenGL ES 2/3).

Listing 14-3. SBGWeapon()(OpenGL ES 1)

```
public class SBGWeapon {

public float posY = 0f;
public float posX = 0f;
public boolean shotFired = false;

private FloatBuffer vertexBuffer;
private FloatBuffer textureBuffer;
private ByteBuffer indexBuffer;

private float vertices[] = {
0.0f, 0.0f, 0.0f,
1.0f, 0.0f, 0.0f,
1.0f, 1.0f, 0.0f,
0.0f, 1.0f, 0.0f,
};

private float texture[] = {
0.0f, 0.0f,
0.25f, 0.0f,
0.25f, 0.25f,
0.0f, 0.25f,
};

private byte indices[] = {
0,1,2,
0,2,3,
};

public SFWeapon() {

ByteBuffer byteBuf = ByteBuffer.allocateDirect(vertices.length * 4);
byteBuf.order(ByteOrder.nativeOrder());
vertexBuffer = byteBuf.asFloatBuffer();
vertexBuffer.put(vertices);
vertexBuffer.position(0);

byteBuf = ByteBuffer.allocateDirect(texture.length * 4);
byteBuf.order(ByteOrder.nativeOrder());
textureBuffer = byteBuf.asFloatBuffer();
textureBuffer.put(texture);
textureBuffer.position(0);

indexBuffer = ByteBuffer.allocateDirect(indices.length);
indexBuffer.put(indices);
indexBuffer.position(0);
}

public void draw(GL10gl, int[] spriteSheet) {
gl.glBindTexture(GL10.GL_TEXTURE_2D, spriteSheet[1]);
```

```java
gl.glFrontFace(GL10.GL_CCW);
gl.glEnable(GL10.GL_CULL_FACE);
gl.glCullFace(GL10.GL_BACK);

gl.glEnableClientState(GL10.GL_VERTEX_ARRAY);
gl.glEnableClientState(GL10.GL_TEXTURE_COORD_ARRAY);

gl.glVertexPointer(3, GL10.GL_FLOAT, 0, vertexBuffer);
gl.glTexCoordPointer(2, GL10.GL_FLOAT, 0, textureBuffer);

gl.glDrawElements(GL10.GL_TRIANGLES, indices.length, GL10.GL_UNSIGNED_BYTE, indexBuffer);

gl.glDisableClientState(GL10.GL_VERTEX_ARRAY);
gl.glDisableClientState(GL10.GL_TEXTURE_COORD_ARRAY);
gl.glDisable(GL10.GL_CULL_FACE);
}

public void loadTexture(GL10gl,int texture, Context context) {
InputStream imagestream = context.getResources().openRawResource(texture);
Bitmap bitmap = null;

Matrix flip = new Matrix();
flip.postScale(-1f, -1f);

try {

bitmap = BitmapFactory.decodeStream(imagestream);

}catch(Exception e){

}finally {
try {
imagestream.close();
imagestream = null;
} catch (IOException e) {
}
}

gl.glGenTextures(1, textures, 0);
gl.glBindTexture(GL10.GL_TEXTURE_2D, textures[0]);

gl.glTexParameterf(GL10.GL_TEXTURE_2D, GL10.GL_TEXTURE_MIN_FILTER, GL10.GL_NEAREST);
gl.glTexParameterf(GL10.GL_TEXTURE_2D, GL10.GL_TEXTURE_MAG_FILTER, GL10.GL_LINEAR);

gl.glTexParameterf(GL10.GL_TEXTURE_2D, GL10.GL_TEXTURE_WRAP_S, GL10.GL_REPEAT);
gl.glTexParameterf(GL10.GL_TEXTURE_2D, GL10.GL_TEXTURE_WRAP_T, GL10.GL_REPEAT);

GLUtils.texImage2D(GL10.GL_TEXTURE_2D, 0, bitmap, 0);

bitmap.recycle();
}

}
```

Listing 14-4. SBGWeapon() (OpenGL ES 2/3)

```java
public class SBGWeapon {

public float posY = 0f;
public float posX = 0f;
public boolean shotFired = false;

private final String vertexShaderCode =
"uniform mat4 uMVPMatrix;" +
"attribute vec4 vPosition;" +
"attribute vec2 TexCoordIn;" +
"varying vec2 TexCoordOut;" +
"void main() {" +
"  gl_Position = uMVPMatrix * vPosition;" +
"  TexCoordOut = TexCoordIn;" +
"}";

private final String fragmentShaderCode =
"precision mediump float;" +
"uniform vec4 vColor;" +
"uniform sampler2D TexCoordIn;" +
"varying vec2 TexCoordOut;" +
"void main() {" +
"  gl_FragColor = texture2D(TexCoordIn, TexCoordOut);" +
"}";

private float texture[] = {
0f, 0f,
1f, 0f,
1f, 1f,
0f, 1f,
};

private int[] textures = new int[1];
private final FloatBuffer vertexBuffer;
private final ShortBuffer drawListBuffer;
private final FloatBuffer textureBuffer;
private final int program;
private int positionHandle;
private int matrixHandle;

static final int COORDS_PER_VERTEX = 3;
static final int COORDS_PER_TEXTURE = 2;
static float vertices[] = { -1f,  1f, 0.0f,
-1f, -1f, 0.0f,
1f, -1f, 0.0f,
1f,  1f, 0.0f };

private final short indices[] = { 0, 1, 2, 0, 2, 3 };
```

```java
private final int vertexStride = COORDS_PER_VERTEX * 4;
public static int textureStride = COORDS_PER_TEXTURE * 4;

public void loadTexture(int texture, Context context) {
InputStream imagestream = context.getResources().openRawResource(texture);
Bitmap bitmap = null;

android.graphics.Matrix flip = new android.graphics.Matrix();
flip.postScale(-1f, -1f);

try {

bitmap = BitmapFactory.decodeStream(imagestream);

}catch(Exception e){

}finally {
try {
imagestream.close();
imagestream = null;
} catch (IOException e) {
}
}

GLES20.glGenTextures(1, textures, 0);
GLES20.glBindTexture(GLES20.GL_TEXTURE_2D, textures[0]);

GLES20.glTexParameterf(GLES20.GL_TEXTURE_2D, GLES20.GL_TEXTURE_MIN_FILTER, GLES20.GL_NEAREST);
GLES20.glTexParameterf(GLES20.GL_TEXTURE_2D, GLES20.GL_TEXTURE_MAG_FILTER, GLES20.GL_LINEAR);

GLES20.glTexParameterf(GLES20.GL_TEXTURE_2D, GLES20.GL_TEXTURE_WRAP_S, GLES20.GL_REPEAT);
GLES20.glTexParameterf(GLES20.GL_TEXTURE_2D, GLES20.GL_TEXTURE_WRAP_T, GLES20.GL_REPEAT);

GLUtils.texImage2D(GLES20.GL_TEXTURE_2D, 0, bitmap, 0);

bitmap.recycle();
}

public SBGWeapon() {

ByteBuffer byteBuff = ByteBuffer.allocateDirect(
byteBuff.order(ByteOrder.nativeOrder());
vertexBuffer = byteBuff.asFloatBuffer();
vertexBuffer.put(vertices);
vertexBuffer.position(0);

byteBuff = ByteBuffer.allocateDirect(texture.length * 4);
byteBuff.order(ByteOrder.nativeOrder());
textureBuffer = byteBuff.asFloatBuffer();
textureBuffer.put(texture);
textureBuffer.position(0);
```

```
ByteBuffer indexBuffer = ByteBuffer.allocateDirect(
indexBuffer.order(ByteOrder.nativeOrder());
drawListBuffer = indexBuffer.asShortBuffer();
drawListBuffer.put(indices);
drawListBuffer.position(0);

int vertexShader = SBGGameRenderer.loadShader(
GLES20.GL_VERTEX_SHADER,vertexShaderCode);
int fragmentShader = SBGGameRenderer.loadShader(
GLES20.GL_FRAGMENT_SHADER,fragmentShaderCode);

program = GLES20.glCreateProgram();
GLES20.glAttachShader(program, vertexShader);
GLES20.glAttachShader(program, fragmentShader);
GLES20.glLinkProgram(program);
}

public void draw(float[] matrix) {

GLES20.glUseProgram(program);

positionHandle = GLES20.glGetAttribLocation(program, "vPosition");

GLES20.glEnableVertexAttribArray(positionHandle);

int vsTextureCoord = GLES20.glGetAttribLocation(program, "TexCoordIn");

GLES20.glVertexAttribPointer(positionHandle, COORDS_PER_VERTEX,
GLES20.GL_FLOAT, false,
vertexStride, vertexBuffer);
GLES20.glVertexAttribPointer(vsTextureCoord, COORDS_PER_TEXTURE,
GLES20.GL_FLOAT, false,
textureStride, textureBuffer);
GLES20.glEnableVertexAttribArray(vsTextureCoord);
GLES20.glActiveTexture(GLES20.GL_TEXTURE0);
GLES20.glBindTexture(GLES20.GL_TEXTURE_2D, textures[0]);
intfsTexture = GLES20.glGetUniformLocation(program, "TexCoordOut");
GLES20.glUniform1i(fsTexture, 0);

matrixHandle = GLES20.glGetUniformLocation(program, "uMVPMatrix");

GLES20.glUniformMatrix4fv(matrixHandle, 1, false, matrix, 0);

GLES20.glDrawElements(GLES20.GL_TRIANGLES, drawOrder.length,
GLES20.GL_UNSIGNED_SHORT, drawListBuffer);

GLES20.glDisableVertexAttribArray(positionHandle);
}
}
```

The SBGWeapon() class contains three key features beyond those required by OpenGL ES. Two variables(x and y) are used to track the on-axis coordinates of the weapon through the game loop. The shotFired variable is used to determine whether the specific instantiation of SBGWeapon has been fired and should be drawn on the screen or ignored.

Why have a Boolean to represent whether the shot has been fired? It is not uncommon for a player in a game to fire multiple shots in quick succession. This means that at any one time, your game could have to track many shots in a single iteration of the game loop. By using the shotFired boolean you can determine which of the SBGWeapons in memory have been fired and which are waiting to be drawn.

The plan from here is to instantiate an SBGWeapon() in your Renderer class. Then, when you detect the PLAYER_FIRE_WEAPON, draw the SBGWeapon() and move it in a straight line on each iteration of the game loop, until the SBGWeapon() hits a target or reaches the end of the screen.

In the Renderer class, instantiate an array of SBGWeapons.In Listings 14-5 and 14-6, I will use an array of four, meaning that only four missiles can be on the screen together at one time.

```
private SBGWeapon[] playerFire = new SBGWeapon[4];
```

Don't forget to load the texture for the image of whatever weapon you are firing. The texture is loaded in the onSurfaceCreated() method of the Renderer (see Listings 14-5 and 14-6).

Listing 14-5. Load the Texture (OpenGL ES 1)

```
for(int x = 0; x<4; x++){
playerFire[x].loadTexture(gl,R.drawable.weapon, context);
}
```

Listing 14-6. Load the Texture (OpenGL ES 2/3)

```
for(int x = 0; x<4; x++){
playerFire[x].loadTexture(R.drawable.weapon, context);
}
```

Finally, create a new method that can be called from the game loop. In many of the solutions in this book, I've referenced a case statement that acts on playerAction. Add a new case to this statement that tests for playerAction = PLAYER_FIRE_WEAPON. If PLAYER_FIRE_WEAPON is detected, call your new method to draw the weapons to the screen (see Listings 14-7 and 14-8).

Listing 14-7. firePlayerWeapon() (OpenGL ES 1)

```
private void firePlayerWeapon(GL10gl){
for(int x = 0; x < 4; x++  ){
if (playerFire[x].shotFired){
int nextShot = 0;
if (playerFire[x].posY> 4.25){ //represents the top of the screen
playerFire[x].shotFired = false;
}else{
if (playerFire[x].posY> 2){
if (x == 3){//since we only have 4 should, recycle any that are no longer in use
nextShot = 0;
}else{
```

```
nextShot = x + 1;
}
if (playerFire[nextShot].shotFired == false){
playerFire[nextShot].shotFired = true;
//set the weapon x to the x of the character when it was fired
playerFire[nextShot].posX = player.x;
playerFire[nextShot].posY = 1.25f;
}


}
playerFire[x].posY += .12f; //the speed of the shot as it moves
gl.glMatrixMode(GL10.GL_MODELVIEW);
gl.glLoadIdentity();
gl.glPushMatrix();
gl.glTranslatef(playerFire[x].posX, playerFire[x].posY, 0f);

gl.glMatrixMode(GL10.GL_TEXTURE);
gl.glLoadIdentity();
gl.glTranslatef(0.0f,0.0f, 0.0f);

playerFire[x].draw(gl);
gl.glPopMatrix();
gl.glLoadIdentity();

}
}
}
}
```

Listing 14-8. firePlayerWeapon() (OpenGL ES 2/3)

```
private void firePlayerWeapon(GL10 unused, float[] rotationMatrix, float[] matrix){
for(int x = 0; x < 4; x++  ){
if (playerFire[x].shotFired){
int nextShot = 0;
if (playerFire[x].posY> 4.25){ //represents the top of the screen
playerFire[x].shotFired = false;
}else{
if (playerFire[x].posY> 2){
if (x == 3){//since we only have 4 should, recycle any that are no longer in use
nextShot = 0;
}else{
nextShot = x + 1;
}
if (playerFire[nextShot].shotFired == false){
playerFire[nextShot].shotFired = true;
//set the weapon x to the x of the character when it was fired
playerFire[nextShot].posX = player.x;
playerFire[nextShot].posY = 1.25f;
}

}
```

```
playerFire[x].posY += .12f; //the speed of the shot as it moves
Matrix.translateM(RotationMatrix, 0, playerFire[x].posX, playerFire[x].posY, 0);
playerFire[x].draw(matrix);
Matrix.multiplyMM(matrix, 0, rotationMatrix, 0, matrix, 0);

          }
      }
   }
}
```

This method will fire a shot from the position of the character, straight up until it hits the top edge of the screen. Modify the assignment of the x and y values of SBGWeapon() to move the shot in different directions. By increasing or decreasing the x value, your shot will move to the right or to the left; by increasing or decreasing the y value, your shot will move up or down.

In Chapter 15, you will be presented with solutions for implementing collision detection. Collision detection is the key to acting when your shot hits a target, rather than simply having your shot move off the edge of the screen.

In the next solution, you will modify the firePlayerWeapon() method to move the shot in a parabolic motion, as if thrown rather than shot straight.

14.3 Animate a Thrown Weapon

Problem

The weapons do not travel in an arc like a thrown weapon would.

Solution

Use a formula, like that used when jumping, to determine a curved trajectory.

How It Works

To move your shot in a arching motion, as if it were thrown, you need to modify the firePlayerWeapon() method. We are going to use the same math formula from Chapter 13 that enabled the character to jump, and place it in the firePlayerWeapons() formula. This is shown in Listings 14-9 and 14-10.

Listing 14-9. Arching Trajectory (OpenGL ES 1)

```
private void firePlayerWeapon(GL10gl){
for(int x = 0; x < 4; x++  ){
if (playerFire[x].shotFired){
int nextShot = 0;

previousArcPos = arcJump;
```

```
arcJump += (float)(((Math.PI / 2) / .5) * PLAYER_RUN_SPEED);
if (arcJump<= Math.PI)
{
playerFire[x].posY += 1.5 / .5 * .15 * PLAYER_RUN_SPEED;

}else{
playerFire[x].posY -=(Math.sin((double)posArc) - Math.sin((double)previousArcPos))* 1.5;
if (playerFire[x].posY<= .75f){
playerFire[x].shotFired = false;
playerFire[x].posY = .75f;
}else{

if (x == 3){//since we only have 4 should, recycle any that are no longer in use
nextShot = 0;
}else{
nextShot = x + 1;
}
}

if (playerFire[nextShot].shotFired == false){
playerFire[nextShot].shotFired = true;
playerFire[nextShot].posX = player.x;
playerFire[nextShot].posY = player.y;
}

}

playerFire[x].posx += .12f;

gl.glMatrixMode(GL10.GL_MODELVIEW);
gl.glLoadIdentity();
gl.glPushMatrix();
gl.glTranslatef(playerFire[x].posX, playerFire[x].posY, 0f);

gl.glMatrixMode(GL10.GL_TEXTURE);
gl.glLoadIdentity();
gl.glTranslatef(0.0f,0.0f, 0.0f);

playerFire[x].draw(gl);
gl.glPopMatrix();
gl.glLoadIdentity();

}
}
}
}
```

Listing 14-10. Arching Trajectory (OpenGL ES 2/3)

```
private void firePlayerWeapon(GL10 unused, float[] rotationMatrix, float[] matrix){
for(int x = 0; x < 4; x++  ){
if (playerFire[x].shotFired){
```

```
int nextShot = 0;
previousArcPos = arcJump;

arcJump += (float)(((Math.PI / 2) / .5) * PLAYER_RUN_SPEED);
if (arcJump<= Math.PI)
{
playerFire[x].posY += 1.5 / .5 * .15 * PLAYER_RUN_SPEED;

}else{
playerFire[x].posY -=(Math.sin((double)posJump) - Math.sin((double)previousJumpPos))* 1.5;
if (playerFire[x].posY<= .75f){
playerFire[x].shotFired = false;
playerFire[x].posY = .75f;
}else{

if (x == 3){//since we only have 4 should, recycle any that are no longer in use
nextShot = 0;
}else{
nextShot = x + 1;
}
}

if (playerFire[nextShot].shotFired == false){
playerFire[nextShot].shotFired = true;
playerFire[nextShot].posX = player.x;
playerFire[nextShot].posY = player.y;
}

}

playerFire[x].posx += .12f;
Matrix.translateM(RotationMatrix, 0, playerFire[x].posX, playerFire[x].posY, 0);
playerFire[x].draw(matrix);
Matrix.multiplyMM(matrix, 0, rotationMatrix, 0, matrix, 0);

}
}
}
}
```

By making this small modification, you can give your weapon a thrown arc rather than the straight line of a projectile that has been fired.

Summary

In Chapter 13 you reviewed recipes that allowed you to add enemies to your game. However, adding enemies to the game is unfair if the player does not have a way to defend themselves. The recipes in this chapter helped you provide the player with a way to fire weapons.

15

Collision Detection

Collision detection is a key component to almost any game and almost every game type. In a game without collision detection, items, obstacles, characters, and weapons would move about the screen and float past each other without any consequence.

Your game code needs to be able to determine if objects that are on the screen touch or cross paths with each other. It is only after you determine that two or more objects are touching that you can then perform actions on them such as applying damage, stopping motion, powering up a character, or destroying an object.

This chapter will cover some solutions that aid you with problems in collision detection. Collision detection can be tricky, but the solutions in this chapter should help to make the process a bit easier.

15.1 Detect Obstacles

Problem

The game character can move through objects on the screen that should stop them.

Solution

Use basic collision detection to determine if the character has touched an obstacle or the edge of the screen.

How It Works

Basic collision detection is useful if you are creating a game where characters are faced with static obstacles such as floors and platforms, the edges of the screen, or steps. You can use constant values when you are testing for the location of static objects. For example, in Recipes 13.1 and 13.2 for making the character jump, I used basic collision detection to determine when the character had finished the jump and was back on the ground, as shown in Listings 15-1 (OpenGL ES 1) and 15-2 (OpenGL ES 2/3).

Listing 15-1. Basic Jumping Collision Detection (OpenGL ES 1)

```
previousJumpPos = posJump;

posJump += (float)(((Math.PI / 2) / .5) * PLAYER_RUN_SPEED);

if (posJump <= Math.PI)
{
goodguy.posY += 1.5 / .5 * .15 * PLAYER_RUN_SPEED;
}else{
goodguy. posY -=(Math.sin((double)posJump) - Math.sin((double)previousJumpPos))* 1.5;
if (goodguy. posY<= .75f){
playeraction = PLAYER_STAND;
goodguy.posY = .75f;
}
}


goodguy. posX += PLAYER_RUN_SPEED;
gl.glMatrixMode(GL10.GL_MODELVIEW);
gl.glLoadIdentity();
gl.glPushMatrix();
gl.glScalef(.15f, .15f, 1f);
gl.glTranslatef(goodguy. posX, goodguy. posY, 0);
gl.glPopMatrix();
gl.glLoadIdentity();
```

Listing 15-2. Basic Jumping Collision Detection (OpenGL ES 2/3)

```
previousJumpPos = posJump;

posJump += (float)(((Math.PI / 2) / .5) * PLAYER_RUN_SPEED);
if (posJump <= Math.PI)
{
goodguy. posY += 1.5 / .5 * .15 * PLAYER_RUN_SPEED;

}else{
goodguy. posY -=(Math.sin((double)posJump) - Math.sin((double)previousJumpPos))* 1.5;
if (goodguy.y<= .75f){
playeraction = PLAYER_STAND;
goodguy.posY = .75f;
}
}
goodguy. posX += PLAYER_RUN_SPEED;
Matrix.translateM(RotationMatrix, 0, goodguy. posX, goodguy. posY, 0);
```

The bolded code in Listings 15-1 and 15-2 illustrates how, in testing that the y position of the character has reached the level of the ground, a constant of .75 is used. Since we know that the ground of the game will always be at .75 on the y axis, this simple form of collision detection can be effective.

What about running off the edge of the screen? If the action of your game needs to be contained to a single screen, and the x axis in OpenGL ES has been scaled to range from 0 (far left) to 4 (far right), you can test your character against that to stop the image from leaving the screen.

```
if(goodguy.posX<= 0 )
{
//the player has reached the left edge of the screen
goodguy. posX = 0; //correct the image's position and perform whatever action is necessary
}
```

This process requires an extra step if you are testing for a collision against the right edge of the screen. The x position of the character in OpenGL ES represents the lower left-hand corner of the image. Therefore, if you are testing whether the image of the character has encountered the right-hand side of the screen, the x position of the character, at the lower left-hand side, will not reach the right edge of the screen until the entire image has already passed off the screen.

You can compensate for this by adding the size of the character image to the if statement that tests for the collision.

```
if(goodguy. posX +.25f>= 4 )
{
//the player has reached the right edge of the screen
goodguy. posX = (4f - .25f); //correct the image's position and
                             //perform whatever action is necessary
}
```

The basic method of collision detection is effective for less complex game logic where there are many static objects, the size and location of which are easily known to the game loop.

What if your game logic is not that easy? The next solution helps you detect collisions between objects that are moving and whose positions are not predictable.

15.2 Detect Collisions Between Multiple Moving Objects

Problem

The game needs to detect whether two or more moving objects have collided with each other.

Solution

Use a looping method to test for collisions on the edges of all OpenGL images.

How It Works

To implement a more robust form of collision detection, create a new method that can be called from your game loop. The method will loop through all of the active items on the screen and determine whether any are colliding.

The key fields needed to implement this kind of collision detection are the x- and y-axis coordinates of the objects' current locations, and the status of the objects. The status of an object refers to whether the object is eligible to be included in collision detection. This could include a flag that the object has already been destroyed, or perhaps the character being tested has a completed an achievement that allows them to be free of collision detection for a specific period of time.

Listings 15-3 and 15-4 depict a class for a character in a game. Three public values have been added to the class: one each for the x- and y-axis coordinates to track the character's current position, and a Boolean to indicate whether the character has already been destroyed.

Listing 15-3. SBGEnemy( ) (OpenGL ES 1)

```
public class SBGEnemy {

public float posY = 0;
public float posX = 0;
public bool isDestroyed = false;

private FloatBuffer vertexBuffer;
private FloatBuffer textureBuffer;
private ByteBufferi ndexBuffer;

private float vertices[] = {
0.0, 0.0, 0.0,
1.0, 0.0, 0.0,
1.0, 1.0, 0.0,
0.0, 1.0, 0.0,
};

private float texture[] = {
0.0, 0.0,
0.25f, 0.0,
0.25f, 0.25f,
0.0, 0.25f,
};

private byte indices[] = {
0,1,2,
0,2,3,
};

public SBGEnemy () {

ByteBuffer byteBuf = ByteBuffer.allocateDirect(vertices.length * 4);
byteBuf.order(ByteOrder.nativeOrder());
vertexBuffer = byteBuf.asFloatBuffer();
vertexBuffer.put(vertices);
vertexBuffer.position(0);

byteBuf = ByteBuffer.allocateDirect(texture.length * 4);
byteBuf.order(ByteOrder.nativeOrder());
textureBuffer = byteBuf.asFloatBuffer();
```

```
textureBuffer.put(texture);
textureBuffer.position(0);

indexBuffer = ByteBuffer.allocateDirect(indices.length);
indexBuffer.put(indices);
indexBuffer.position(0);
}

public void draw(GL10gl, int[] spriteSheet) {
gl.glBindTexture(GL10.GL_TEXTURE_2D, spriteSheet[1]);

gl.glFrontFace(GL10.GL_CCW);
gl.glEnable(GL10.GL_CULL_FACE);
gl.glCullFace(GL10.GL_BACK);

gl.glEnableClientState(GL10.GL_VERTEX_ARRAY);
gl.glEnableClientState(GL10.GL_TEXTURE_COORD_ARRAY);

gl.glVertexPointer(3, GL10.GL_FLOAT, 0, vertexBuffer);
gl.glTexCoordPointer(2, GL10.GL_FLOAT, 0, textureBuffer);

gl.glDrawElements(GL10.GL_TRIANGLES, indices.length, GL10.GL_UNSIGNED_BYTE, indexBuffer);

gl.glDisableClientState(GL10.GL_VERTEX_ARRAY);
gl.glDisableClientState(GL10.GL_TEXTURE_COORD_ARRAY);
gl.glDisable(GL10.GL_CULL_FACE);
}

public void loadTexture(GL10gl,int texture, Context context) {
InputStream imagestream = context.getResources().openRawResource(texture);
Bitmap bitmap = null;

Matrix flip = new Matrix();
flip.postScale(-1f, -1f);

try {

bitmap = BitmapFactory.decodeStream(imagestream);

}catch(Exception e){

}finally {
try {
imagestream.close();
imagestream = null;
} catch (IOException e) {
}
}

gl.glGenTextures(1, textures, 0);
gl.glBindTexture(GL10.GL_TEXTURE_2D, textures[0]);
```

```
gl.glTexParameterf(GL10.GL_TEXTURE_2D, GL10.GL_TEXTURE_MIN_FILTER, GL10.GL_NEAREST);
gl.glTexParameterf(GL10.GL_TEXTURE_2D, GL10.GL_TEXTURE_MAG_FILTER, GL10.GL_LINEAR);

gl.glTexParameterf(GL10.GL_TEXTURE_2D, GL10.GL_TEXTURE_WRAP_S, GL10.GL_REPEAT);
gl.glTexParameterf(GL10.GL_TEXTURE_2D, GL10.GL_TEXTURE_WRAP_T, GL10.GL_REPEAT);

GLUtils.texImage2D(GL10.GL_TEXTURE_2D, 0, bitmap, 0);

bitmap.recycle();
    }

}
```

Listing 15-4. SBGEnemy( ) (OpenGL ES 2/3)

```
public class SBGEnemy {

public float posY = 0;
public float posX = 0;
public bool isDestroyed = false;

private final String vertexShaderCode =
"uniform mat4 uMVPMatrix;" +
"attribute vec4 vPosition;" +
"attribute vec2 TexCoordIn;" +
"varying vec2 TexCoordOut;" +
"void main() {" +
"  gl_Position = uMVPMatrix * vPosition;" +
"  TexCoordOut = TexCoordIn;" +
"}";

private final String fragmentShaderCode =
"precision mediump float;" +
"uniform vec4 vColor;" +
"uniform sampler2D TexCoordIn;" +
"varying vec2 TexCoordOut;" +
"void main() {" +
"  gl_FragColor = texture2D(TexCoordIn, TexCoordOut);" +
"}";

private float texture[] = {
0, 0,
1f, 0,
1f, 1f,
0, 1f,
};

private int[] textures = new int[1];
private final FloatBuffer vertexBuffer;
private final ShortBuffer drawListBuffer;
private final FloatBuffer textureBuffer;
private final int program;
```

```
private int positionHandle;
private int matrixHandle;

static final int COORDS_PER_VERTEX = 3;
static final int COORDS_PER_TEXTURE = 2;
static float vertices[] = { -1f,  1f, 0.0,
-1f, -1f, 0.0,
1f, -1f, 0.0,
1f,  1f, 0.0 };

private final short indices[] = { 0, 1, 2, 0, 2, 3 };

private final int vertexStride = COORDS_PER_VERTEX * 4;
public static int textureStride = COORDS_PER_TEXTURE * 4;

public void loadTexture(int texture, Context context) {
InputStream imagestream = context.getResources().openRawResource(texture);
      Bitmap bitmap = null;

android.graphics.Matrix flip = new android.graphics.Matrix();
flip.postScale(-1f, -1f);

try {

bitmap = BitmapFactory.decodeStream(imagestream);

}catch(Exception e){

}finally {
try {
imagestream.close();
imagestream = null;
} catch (IOException e) {
}
}

GLES20.glGenTextures(1, textures, 0);
GLES20.glBindTexture(GLES20.GL_TEXTURE_2D, textures[0]);

GLES20.glTexParameterf(GLES20.GL_TEXTURE_2D, GLES20.GL_TEXTURE_MIN_FILTER,
GLES20.GL_NEAREST);
GLES20.glTexParameterf(GLES20.GL_TEXTURE_2D, GLES20.GL_TEXTURE_MAG_FILTER,
GLES20.GL_LINEAR);

GLES20.glTexParameterf(GLES20.GL_TEXTURE_2D, GLES20.GL_TEXTURE_WRAP_S, GLES20.GL_REPEAT);
GLES20.glTexParameterf(GLES20.GL_TEXTURE_2D, GLES20.GL_TEXTURE_WRAP_T, GLES20.GL_REPEAT);

GLUtils.texImage2D(GLES20.GL_TEXTURE_2D, 0, bitmap, 0);

bitmap.recycle();
}
```

```java
public SBGEnemy () {

ByteBuffer byteBuff = ByteBuffer.allocateDirect(
byteBuff.order(ByteOrder.nativeOrder());
vertexBuffer = byteBuff.asFloatBuffer();
vertexBuffer.put(vertices);
vertexBuffer.position(0);

byteBuff = ByteBuffer.allocateDirect(texture.length * 4);
byteBuff.order(ByteOrder.nativeOrder());
textureBuffer = byteBuff.asFloatBuffer();
textureBuffer.put(texture);
textureBuffer.position(0);

ByteBuffer indexBuffer = ByteBuffer.allocateDirect(
indexBuffer.order(ByteOrder.nativeOrder());
drawListBuffer = indexBuffer.asShortBuffer();
drawListBuffer.put(indices);
drawListBuffer.position(0);

int vertexShader = SBGGameRenderer.loadShader(
GLES20.GL_VERTEX_SHADER,vertexShaderCode);
int fragmentShader = SBGGameRenderer.loadShader(
GLES20.GL_FRAGMENT_SHADER, fragmentShaderCode);

program = GLES20.glCreateProgram();
GLES20.glAttachShader(program, vertexShader);
GLES20.glAttachShader(program, fragmentShader);
GLES20.glLinkProgram(program);
}

public void draw(float[] matrix) {

GLES20.glUseProgram(program);

positionHandle = GLES20.glGetAttribLocation(program, "vPosition");

GLES20.glEnableVertexAttribArray(positionHandle);

int vsTextureCoord = GLES20.glGetAttribLocation(program, "TexCoordIn");

GLES20.glVertexAttribPointer(positionHandle, COORDS_PER_VERTEX,
GLES20.GL_FLOAT, false,
vertexStride, vertexBuffer);
GLES20.glVertexAttribPointer(vsTextureCoord, COORDS_PER_TEXTURE,
GLES20.GL_FLOAT, false,
textureStride, textureBuffer);
GLES20.glEnableVertexAttribArray(vsTextureCoord);
GLES20.glActiveTexture(GLES20.GL_TEXTURE0);
GLES20.glBindTexture(GLES20.GL_TEXTURE_2D, textures[0]);
```

```
int fsTexture = GLES20.glGetUniformLocation(program, "TexCoordOut");
GLES20.glUniform1i(fsTexture, 0);

matrixHandle = GLES20.glGetUniformLocation(program, "uMVPMatrix");

GLES20.glUniformMatrix4fv(matrixHandle, 1, false, matrix, 0);

GLES20.glDrawElements(GLES20.GL_TRIANGLES, drawOrder.length,
GLES20.GL_UNSIGNED_SHORT, drawListBuffer);

GLES20.glDisableVertexAttribArray(positionHandle);
}
}
```

Now, build a new class that can be called from the game loop. In Chapter 14, a solution was presented where the player could fire weapons. The weapons that were fired were in an array, allowing four shots to be active on the screen at one time. We are going to build upon this by looping through each of the four shots, checking whether they are actively fired, and then checking whether they have collided with the enemy character in the previous code listing.

The easiest way to accomplish the collision test is to create (in memory) a bounding box around each active object and then test whether the edge of any two objects' bounding boxes collide. Why bounding boxes? It is easier to test straight lines, such as box edges, than to try to calculate the true edges of very complex shapes. Also, objects in the game will typically collide so quickly that the eye will not be able to detect that the collision occurred a fraction of a millimeter away from the visible border of the actual object.

Create the bounding box by adding the size (in coordinates) to the current x- and y-coordinate position of the object. This means that an object that is scaled to .25 square on the coordinate axis will have a bounding box from x to (x + .25), and from y to (y + .25). Anything that crosses into that space will collide with that object. To test for a collision in this example, all you need to do is check whether another object's bounding box contains a point that is between (x to (x + .25)) and (y to (y + .25)). If so, those two objects have collided.

In Listing 15-5, the shot being fired has .25 coordinate value bounding box, and the enemy has a 1 coordinate value bounding box.

Listing 15-5. Detecting the bounding box

```
private void detectCollisions(){
for (int y = 1; y < 4; y ++){ //loop through the 4 potential shots in the array
if (playerFire[y].shotFired){ //only test the shots that are currently active
if(!enemy.isDestroyed){
//only test the shot against the enemy if it is not already destroyed
//test for the collision
if ((((playerFire[y].posY  >= enemy.posY
&& playerFire[y].posY <= enemy.posY + 1f )  ||
(playerFire[y].posY +.25f>= enemy.posY
&& playerFire[y].posY + .25f<= enemy.posY + 1f )) &&
((playerFire[y].posX>= enemy.posX
```

```
&& playerFire[y].posX<= enemy.posX + 1f) ||
(playerFire[y].posX + .25f>= enemy.posX
&& playerFire[y].posX + 25f<= enemy.posX + 1f ))){
//collision detected between enemy and a shot
}
}
}
}
}
```

This method works well when detecting a collision between a round of shots and a single enemy. To test for a collision between a round of shots and a number of enemies, you will need to modify the method slightly to loop through your array of enemies (see Listing 15-6).

Listing 15-6. Loop through the enemies

```
private void detectCollisions(){
for (int y = 1; y < 4; y ++){
if (playerFire[y].shotFired){
for (int x = 1; x < 10; x++ ){ //assumes you have an array of 10 enemies
if(!enemies[x].isDestroyed){
if (((playerFire[y].posY  >= enemies[x].posY
&& playerFire[y].posY <= enemies[x].posY + 1f )  ||
(playerFire[y].posY +.25f>= enemies[x].posY
&& playerFire[y].posY + .25f<= enemies[x].posY + 1f ))
&&  ((playerFire[y].posX>= enemies[x].posX
&& playerFire[y].posX<= enemies[x].posX + 1f) ||
(playerFire[y].posX + .25f>= enemies[x].posX
&& playerFire[y].posX + 25f<= enemies[x].posX + 1f ))){

//collision detected between enemy and a shot

}
}
}
}
}
}
```

This collision detection method will help you test for collisions between the bounding boxes of multiple objects in your game. Once you have detected a collision, you can then act on that collision in the commented area. One of the actions you might want to take is to change the trajectory of an object—as in the instance of a ball bouncing off of a wall.

The next recipe will cover changing an object's trajectory.

15.3 Change Object Trajectory

Problem

A game object, such as a ball, does not change direction when it hits a wall.

Solution

Use collision detection to change the trajectory of an object when it collides with another.

How It Works

There are game types where objects do not necessarily stop or explode when they collide with other objects. Some games, such as breakout-style brick smashers, contain objects that bounce off one another when they collide.

The modification of the detectCollisions() method in this solution helps you detect a collision between two objects (in this case, a ball and a brick) and change the trajectory of the ball on contact.

The code in Listing 15-7 came directly from an old brick-smashing game I wrote, I have left in the code that cycles through the bricks to help you. In the sample, ball is an instantiation of a Ball() class that is identical to the SBGEnemy() class we saw earlier in this chapter. Also, wall is a class that contains within it a collection of rows. Rows are then a collection of instantiated bricks, the class for which is also identical to the SBGEnemy(). This creates a wall for the player to break through that is made up of rows of bricks.

Finally, Listing 15-7 not only checks for collisions between the ball and bricks, but also the ball and the edges of the screen. If the ball hits the edge of the screen, it will bounce off, causing the trajectory to change and keeping the ball in play.

Listing 15-7. detectCollisions()

```
private void detectCollisions(){
if(ball.posY<= 0){
}
for (int x = 0; x <wall.rows.length; x++)
{ //cycle through each brick and see if the ball has collided with it
for(int y = 0; y <wall.rows[x].bricks.length; y++)
{
if(!wall.rows[x].bricks[y].isDestroyed)
{
if (((ball.posY>wall.rows[x].bricks[y].posY - .25f)  //the height of the brick is .25
&& (ball.posY<wall.rows[x].bricks[y].posY)
&& (ball.posX + .25f>wall.rows[x].bricks[y].posX)
&& (ball.posX<wall.rows[x].bricks[y].posX + 1.50))) //the legnthof the brick
{ //there is a collision, destroy the brick and change the trajectory
//of the ball
```

```
wall.rows[x].bricks[y].isDestroyed = true;
//change the trajectory by inverting the y axis
ballTargetY = ballTargetY * -1f;

//if the ball was originally moving to the left when it collided, move it to
//the right after the bounce - otherwise move it to the left
if(ballTargetX == -2f){
ballTargetX = 5f;
}else{
ballTargetX = -2f;
}


}
}


}
}


//Now check for collisions with the player's "paddle" and bounce the ball off accordingly
if((ball.posY - .25f<= .5f)
&& (ball.posX + .25f>player.PosX ) //the paddle has the same dimensions as a brick,
                                //keep it simple
&& (ball.posX<player.PosX  + 1.50)){
//collision detected, change the Y trajectory of the ball, and the direction on the x axis
ballTargetY = ballTargetY * -1f;
if(ballTargetX == -2f){
ballTargetX = 5f;
}else{
ballTargetX = -2f;
}
}

//check for collision with edge of the screeen, change the x axis trajectory on impact
if(ball.posX< 0 || ball.posX + .25f>3.75f)
{
ballTargetX = ballTargetX * -1f;

}

}
```

15.4 Damage Objects upon Collision and Remove Destroyed Objects

Problem

The game does not "damage" objects after collisions. Also, once objects are damaged, they are still visible in the game.

Solution

Use a class to track object damage and remove destroyed objects.

How It Works

In Recipe 15.2, an isDestroyed flag was set to indicate that the object has collided with another and should be destroyed, thus removing it from the game. This is one way to track whether an object has been destroyed. But what if you want to create a system whereby an object can be hit (collision) multiple times before being destroyed?

Modify the objects class. Reference the SBGEnemy() class from Listing 15-1 to include a damageCounter.

```
public class SBGEnemy {

public float posY = 0;
public float posX = 0;
public bool isDestroyed = false;
public int damageCounter = 0;
...
}
```

Now, on collision increment the damage counter by one. Set the isDestroyed flag if the counter reaches a predetermined threshold.

```
private void detectCollisions(){

...

//collision detected
character.damageCounter += 1;
if(character.damageCounter == 3){
character.isDestroyed = true;
}

...
}
```

With the character "destroyed," the final step is to remove it from the screen. The easiest way to do that is to simply not draw it. In your game loop, test that a character or object is not destroyed before drawing it.

```
1f(!character.isDestroyed){
character.draw(gl);
}
```

Chapter 16

Keeping Score

To this point in the book, many problems have been addressed pertaining to Android game development. From moving characters to collision detection, your game should be shaping up nicely. However, one fundamental problem has yet to be addressed: how do you keep score?

Scoring is an integral part of most games. Without a score, the player would have no way to determine how well they are progressing in the game and no way to compare their progress with that of other players. From the earliest days of video games, scores have been the center of many players' bragging rights.

In this chapter, I will present solutions to some common problems related to keeping the score in a game. The solutions should be adaptable to most game types.

16.1 Assign Point Values to Objects

Problem

The game does not award a score to the player for destroying objects.

Solution

Modify an object's class to assign it a score.

How It Works

This solution involves assigning point values to objects, and using those values as a score for the player. Assigning a value to an object in the game is very easy and only requires the modification of the object's class.

In a game, objects can be anything that you want to assign a value to. For example, enemies, breakable objects, and on-screen goals (such as waypoints in levels) can all be assigned a point value that is then used to compute the player's score.

To assign a point value to an enemy, modify the enemy's class to add a property called pointValue. In this example we are going to modify the SBGEnemy() class, used multiple times in this book, and assign it a point value of 3.

```
public class SBGEnemy {
public boolean isDead = false;

public int pointValue = 3;
...


}
```

This same solution can be applied to all of the classes in your game, assigning each a point value that can then be used in the overall score of the game.

Another way this solution can be implemented is in a graduating format. For example, we can use one class to create multiple objects, each with a different point value. Take a look at the following class. This class is taken from a Breakout-style game that I wrote where one brick class was used to create five different kinds of brick.

The class is written in OpenGL ES 1;however, the OpenGL ES code is not important to the solution. Do not worry if your game is in OpenGL ES 2/3, as the modifications that are made to this class are not OpenGL ES version-specific and can be easily followed.

Listing 16-1. PBBrick()

```
public class PBBrick {

public float posY = 0f;
public float posX = 0f;
public float posT = 0f;

public boolean isDestroyed = false;

public int brickType = 0;

private FloatBuffer vertexBuffer;
private FloatBuffer textureBuffer;
private ByteBuffer indexBuffer;

private float vertices[] = {
0.0f, 0.0f, 0.0f,
1.0f, 0.0f, 0.0f,
1.0f, .25f, 0.0f,
0.0f, .25f, 0.0f,
};

private float texture[] = {
0.0f, 0.0f,
```

```
0.25f, 0.0f,
0.25f, 0.25f,
0.0f, 0.25f,
};

private byte indices[] = {
0,1,2,
0,2,3,
};

public PBBrick(int type) {
brickType = type;

ByteBuffer byteBuf = ByteBuffer.allocateDirect(vertices.length * 4);
byteBuf.order(ByteOrder.nativeOrder());
vertexBuffer = byteBuf.asFloatBuffer();
vertexBuffer.put(vertices);
vertexBuffer.position(0);

byteBuf = ByteBuffer.allocateDirect(texture.length * 4);
byteBuf.order(ByteOrder.nativeOrder());
textureBuffer = byteBuf.asFloatBuffer();
textureBuffer.put(texture);
textureBuffer.position(0);

indexBuffer = ByteBuffer.allocateDirect(indices.length);
indexBuffer.put(indices);
indexBuffer.position(0);
}

public void draw(GL10gl, int[] spriteSheet) {
gl.glBindTexture(GL10.GL_TEXTURE_2D, spriteSheet[0]);

gl.glFrontFace(GL10.GL_CCW);
gl.glEnable(GL10.GL_CULL_FACE);
gl.glCullFace(GL10.GL_BACK);

gl.glEnableClientState(GL10.GL_VERTEX_ARRAY);
gl.glEnableClientState(GL10.GL_TEXTURE_COORD_ARRAY);

gl.glVertexPointer(3, GL10.GL_FLOAT, 0, vertexBuffer);
gl.glTexCoordPointer(2, GL10.GL_FLOAT, 0, textureBuffer);

gl.glDrawElements(GL10.GL_TRIANGLES, indices.length, GL10.GL UNSIGNED BYTE, indexBuffer);

gl.glDisableClientState(GL10.GL_VERTEX_ARRAY);
gl.glDisableClientState(GL10.GL_TEXTURE_COORD_ARRAY);
gl.glDisable(GL10.GL_CULL_FACE);
}

}
```

Let's modify this class so that the five different types of bricks are each assigned a different point value ranging from 1 to 5.

Listing 16-2. PBBrick() Modification

```
public class PBBrick {

public float posY = 0f;
public float posX = 0f;
public float posT = 0f;

public boolean isDestroyed = false;

public int brickType = 0;

public int pointValue = 0;

private FloatBuffer vertexBuffer;
private FloatBuffer textureBuffer;
private ByteBuffer indexBuffer;

private float vertices[] = {
0.0f, 0.0f, 0.0f,
1.0f, 0.0f, 0.0f,
1.0f, .25f, 0.0f,
0.0f, .25f, 0.0f,
};

private float texture[] = {
0.0f, 0.0f,
0.25f, 0.0f,
0.25f, 0.25f,
0.0f, 0.25f,
};

private byte indices[] = {
0,1,2,
0,2,3,
};

public PBBrick(int type) {
brickType = type;

switch(type){
case 1:
pointValue = 1;
break;
case 2:
pointValue = 2;
break;
```

```
case 3:
pointValue = 3;
break;
case 4:
pointValue = 4;
break;
case 5:
pointValue = 5;
break;

}

ByteBuffer byteBuf = ByteBuffer.allocateDirect(vertices.length * 4);
byteBuf.order(ByteOrder.nativeOrder());
vertexBuffer = byteBuf.asFloatBuffer();
vertexBuffer.put(vertices);
vertexBuffer.position(0);

byteBuf = ByteBuffer.allocateDirect(texture.length * 4);
byteBuf.order(ByteOrder.nativeOrder());
textureBuffer = byteBuf.asFloatBuffer();
textureBuffer.put(texture);
textureBuffer.position(0);

indexBuffer = ByteBuffer.allocateDirect(indices.length);
indexBuffer.put(indices);
indexBuffer.position(0);
}

...

}
```

In Recipe 16.2, you will take the point values assigned to game objects and use them to create the player's score.

16.2 Add and Track the Score

Problem

The game does not track the player's score, even though each object is assigned a point value.

Solution

Use the game character's class to track the overall score.

How It Works

In this solution, you are going modify the class for the player's character to add a property. The property will be used to track the player's overall score. Once the player character class is modified, you will modify the collision detection method to assign the correct point values to the new score property.

First, modify the player character class and add a new property called overallScore.

```
public class SuperBanditGuy {
public boolean isDead = false;

public int overallScore = 0;
...

}
```

In Chapter 15, you created a method for performing collision detection. Since this solution assumes that the basis for rewarding points will be some kind of collision (e.g., destroying an object), you will modify the collision detection method to assign points when necessary.

Listing 16-3. detectCollisions()

```
private void detectCollisions(){
for (int y = 1; y <4; y ++){
if (playerFire[y].shotFired){
for (int x = 1; x <10; x++ ){ //assumes you have an array of 10 enemies
if(!enemies[x].isDestroyed){
if (((playerFire[y].posY>= enemies[x].posY
&& playerFire[y].posY<= enemies[x].posY + 1f )  ||
(playerFire[y].posY +.25f>= enemies[x].posY
&& playerFire[y].posY + .25f<= enemies[x].posY + 1f )) &&
((playerFire[y].posX>= enemies[x].posX
&& playerFire[y].posX<= enemies[x].posX + 1f) ||
(playerFire[y].posX + .25f>= enemies[x].posX
&& playerFire[y].posX + 25f<= enemies[x].posX + 1f ))){

//collision detected between enemy and a shot
goodguy.overallScore += enemies[x].pointValue;

}
}
}
}
}
}
```

As mentioned, this method was taken from Chapter 15. It is a basic method that tracks collisions on ten different enemies. The enemies[] array is an array of SBGEnemy() classes. The goodguy in the method is simply an instantiation of the SuperBanditGuy() class.

Using this solution, the overall score of the player character will be added to every time they destroy an enemy.

16.3 Write the Score to the Screen

Problem

The game does not display the player's score to the screen.

Solution

Use multiple OpenGL shapes and a sprite sheet to display the score to the user.

How It Works

To track the score, add a new sprite sheet to the project that contains all of the digits used to display the score. This spritesheet can be seen in Figure 16-1.

Figure 16-1. Score digits spritesheet

Next, create a new class called SBGScoreTile(). This class will be used to display a portrait-oriented score tile to the screen in both OpenGL ES 1 and OpenGL ES 2/3 (see Listings 16-4 and 16-5). Later, you will use a sprite sheet to display a specific score digit on the tile.

Listing 16-4. SBGScoreTile() (OpenGL ES 1)

```
public class SBGScoreTile {

private FloatBuffer vertexBuffer;
private FloatBuffer textureBuffer;
private ByteBuffer indexBuffer;

private float vertices[] = {
0.0f, 0.0f, 0.0f,
0.25f, 0.0f, 0.0f,
0.25f, 1.0f, 0.0f,
0.0f, 1.0f, 0.0f,
};
```

```java
private float texture[] = {
0.0f, 0.0f,
0.25f, 0.0f,
0.25f, 0.25f,
0.0f, 0.25f,
};

private byte indices[] = {
0,1,2,
0,2,3,
};

public SBGScoreTile() {

ByteBuffer byteBuf = ByteBuffer.allocateDirect(vertices.length * 4);
byteBuf.order(ByteOrder.nativeOrder());
vertexBuffer = byteBuf.asFloatBuffer();
vertexBuffer.put(vertices);
vertexBuffer.position(0);

byteBuf = ByteBuffer.allocateDirect(texture.length * 4);
byteBuf.order(ByteOrder.nativeOrder());
textureBuffer = byteBuf.asFloatBuffer();
textureBuffer.put(texture);
textureBuffer.position(0);

indexBuffer = ByteBuffer.allocateDirect(indices.length);
indexBuffer.put(indices);
indexBuffer.position(0);
}

public void draw(GL10gl) {
gl.glBindTexture(GL10.GL_TEXTURE_2D, spriteSheet[0]);

gl.glFrontFace(GL10.GL_CCW);
gl.glEnable(GL10.GL_CULL_FACE);
gl.glCullFace(GL10.GL_BACK);

gl.glEnableClientState(GL10.GL_VERTEX_ARRAY);
gl.glEnableClientState(GL10.GL_TEXTURE_COORD_ARRAY);

gl.glVertexPointer(3, GL10.GL_FLOAT, 0, vertexBuffer);
gl.glTexCoordPointer(2, GL10.GL_FLOAT, 0, textureBuffer);

gl.glDrawElements(GL10.GL_TRIANGLES, indices.length, GL10.GL_UNSIGNED_BYTE, indexBuffer);

gl.glDisableClientState(GL10.GL_VERTEX_ARRAY);
gl.glDisableClientState(GL10.GL_TEXTURE_COORD_ARRAY);
gl.glDisable(GL10.GL_CULL_FACE);
}

}
```

Listing 16-5. SBGScoreTile()(OpenGL ES 2/3)

```java
public class SBGScoreTile {

public float scoreX = 0;
public float scoreY = 0;

private final String vertexShaderCode =
"uniform mat4 uMVPMatrix;" +
"attribute vec4 vPosition;" +
"attribute vec2 TexCoordIn;" +
"varying vec2 TexCoordOut;" +
"void main() {" +
"  gl_Position = uMVPMatrix * vPosition;" +
"  TexCoordOut = TexCoordIn;" +
"}";

private final String fragmentShaderCode =
"precision mediump float;" +
"uniform vec4 vColor;" +
"uniform sampler2D TexCoordIn;" +
"uniform float scoreX;" +
"uniform float scoreY;" +
"varying vec2 TexCoordOut;" +
"void main() {" +
" gl_FragColor = texture2D(TexCoordIn, vec2(TexCoordOut.x +
scoreX,TexCoordOut.y + scoreY));"+
"}";

private float texture[] = {
0f, 0f,
1f, 0f,
1f, 1f,
0f, 1f,
};

private int[] textures = new int[1];
private final FloatBuffer vertexBuffer;
private final ShortBuffer drawListBuffer;
private final FloatBuffer textureBuffer;
private final int program;
private int positionHandle;
private int matrixHandle;

static final int COORDS_PER_VERTEX = 3;
static final int COORDS_PER_TEXTURE = 2;
static float vertices[] = { -1f,  1f, 0.0f,
-1f, -1f, 0.0f,
1f, -1f, 0.0f,
1f,  1f, 0.0f };

private final short indices[] = { 0, 1, 2, 0, 2, 3 };
```

```java
private final int vertexStride = COORDS_PER_VERTEX * 4;
public static int textureStride = COORDS_PER_TEXTURE * 4;

public void loadTexture(int texture, Context context) {
InputStream imagestream = context.getResources().openRawResource(texture);
      Bitmap bitmap = null;

android.graphics.Matrix flip = new android.graphics.Matrix();
flip.postScale(-1f, -1f);

try {

bitmap = BitmapFactory.decodeStream(imagestream);

}catch(Exception e){

}finally {
try {
imagestream.close();
imagestream = null;
} catch (IOException e) {
}
}

GLES20.glGenTextures(1, textures, 0);
GLES20.glBindTexture(GLES20.GL_TEXTURE_2D, textures[0]);

GLES20.glTexParameterf(GLES20.GL_TEXTURE_2D, GLES20.GL_TEXTURE_MIN_FILTER,
GLES20.GL_NEAREST);
GLES20.glTexParameterf(GLES20.GL_TEXTURE_2D, GLES20.GL_TEXTURE_MAG_FILTER,
GLES20.GL_LINEAR);

GLES20.glTexParameterf(GLES20.GL_TEXTURE_2D, GLES20.GL_TEXTURE_WRAP_S, GLES20.GL_REPEAT);
GLES20.glTexParameterf(GLES20.GL_TEXTURE_2D, GLES20.GL_TEXTURE_WRAP_T, GLES20.GL_REPEAT);

GLUtils.texImage2D(GLES20.GL_TEXTURE_2D, 0, bitmap, 0);

bitmap.recycle();

}

public SBGScoreTile() {

ByteBuffer byteBuff = ByteBuffer.allocateDirect(
byteBuff.order(ByteOrder.nativeOrder());
vertexBuffer = byteBuff.asFloatBuffer();
vertexBuffer.put(vertices);
vertexBuffer.position(0);

byteBuff = ByteBuffer.allocateDirect(texture.length * 4);
byteBuff.order(ByteOrder.nativeOrder());
textureBuffer = byteBuff.asFloatBuffer();
textureBuffer.put(texture);
textureBuffer.position(0);
```

```
ByteBuffer indexBuffer = ByteBuffer.allocateDirect(
indexBuffer.order(ByteOrder.nativeOrder()));
drawListBuffer = indexBuffer.asShortBuffer();
drawListBuffer.put(indices);
drawListBuffer.position(0);

int vertexShader = SBGGameRenderer.loadShader(
GLES20.GL_VERTEX_SHADER,vertexShaderCode);
int fragmentShader = SBGGameRenderer.loadShader(
GLES20.GL_FRAGMENT_SHADER, fragmentShaderCode);

program = GLES20.glCreateProgram();
GLES20.glAttachShader(program, vertexShader);
GLES20.glAttachShader(program, fragmentShader);
GLES20.glLinkProgram(program);
}

public void draw(float[] matrix) {

GLES20.glUseProgram(mProgram);

mPositionHandle = GLES20.glGetAttribLocation(mProgram, "vPosition");

GLES20.glEnableVertexAttribArray(mPositionHandle);

int vsTextureCoord = GLES20.glGetAttribLocation(mProgram, "TexCoordIn");
GLES20.glVertexAttribPointer(mPositionHandle, COORDS_PER_VERTEX,
GLES20.GL_FLOAT, false, vertexStride, vertexBuffer);
GLES20.glVertexAttribPointer(vsTextureCoord, COORDS_PER_TEXTURE,
GLES20.GL_FLOAT, false, textureStride, textureBuffer);
GLES20.glEnableVertexAttribArray(vsTextureCoord);
GLES20.glActiveTexture(GLES20.GL_TEXTURE0);
GLES20.glBindTexture(GLES20.GL_TEXTURE_2D, textures[0]);
int fsTexture = GLES20.glGetUniformLocation(mProgram, "TexCoordOut");
int fsScoreX = GLES20.glGetUniformLocation(mProgram, "scoreX");
int fsScoreY = GLES20.glGetUniformLocation(mProgram, "scoreY");
GLES20.glUniform1i(fsTexture, 0);
GLES20.glUniform1f(fsScoreX, scoreX);
GLES20.glUniform1f(fsScoreY, scoreY);
mMVPMatrixHandle = GLES20.glGetUniformLocation(mProgram, "uMVPMatrix");

GLES20.glUniformMatrix4fv(mMVPMatrixHandle, 1, false, mvpMatrix, 0);

GLES20.glDrawElements(GLES20.GL_TRIANGLES, drawOrder.length,
GLES20.GL_UNSIGNED_SHORT, drawListBuffer);

GLES20.glDisableVertexAttribArray(mPositionHandle);
}
}
```

Each tile should default to the 0 when drawn. This is accomplished in Listing 16-6 by performing a glTranslatef() to the coordinates of 0,0,0 in the texture matrix in OpenGL ES 1, and indirectly setting the TexCoordOut.x of the fragment shader to 0 in OpenGL ES 2/3 (for a more detailed look at how sprite sheets work see Chapter 6, "Loading a Sprite Sheet").

Listing 16-6. Drawing the Tile (OpenGL ES 1)

```
gl.glMatrixMode(GL10.GL_TEXTURE);
gl.glLoadIdentity();
gl.glTranslatef(0.0f, 0.0f , 0.0f);
```

Listing 16-7. Drawing the Tile (OpenGL ES 2/3)

```
SBGScoreTile.scoreX = 0;
SBGScoreTile.scoreY = 0;
```

Simply advance the sprite sheet to the correct digit for the score. First, create a switch...case statement to set the x and y sprite sheet coordinate location for each corresponding digit.

Listing 16-8. Tile switch Statement

```
switch(SuperBanditGuy){
case 0:
x = 0;
y = 0;
break;
case 1:
x = 0;
y = .25;
break;
case 2:
x = 0;
y = .50;
break;
case 3:
x = 0;
y = .75;
break;

...

}
```

Finally, use the x and y coordinates that are set in the switch statement to display the correct tile.

Listing 16-9. Display the Tile (OpenGL ES 1)

```
gl.glMatrixMode(GL10.GL_TEXTURE);
gl.glLoadIdentity();
gl.glTranslatef(x, y ,0.0f);
```

Listing 16-10. Display the Tile (OpenGL ES 2/3)

```
SBGScoreTile.scoreX = x;
SBGScoreTile.scoreY = y;
```

Chapter 17

Keeping Time

Some games, perhaps the one you are developing, are time based. This could mean that a specific challenge in a game has a time limit in which it needs to be completed, or that the entire game itself can only be played for a predetermined amount of time.

The solutions in this chapter will help you create a timer within your game. You will then use that timer to write to the screen, and to exit the game action after expiration. The key component for tracking time within a game is the Android class `CountDownTimer()`. The `CountDownTimer()` is a very powerful, yet easy to implement, tool.

17.1 Track Time Within the Game

Problem

The user should only have a set amount of time to complete a task.

Solution

Use a `CountDownTimer()` in your game to track the amount of time expired.

How It Works

The key behind establishing a timer is to instantiate a `CountDownTimer()`. The `CountDownTimer()` class is a core Android class, and is not dependent upon OpenGL ES. This means that regardless of whether your game is using OpenGL ES 1, 2, or 3, you can easily use the `CountDownTimer()` in your game. Therefore, the examples in this chapter are OpenGL ES version independent.

The first step is to instantiate the class.

```
newCountDownTimer(millisecondsInFuture, countDownInterval) {
}
```

The constructor of the CountDownTime() takes two parameters. The first parameter, millisecondsInFuture, is the overall duration of the timer, in milliseconds. If you want the timer to last for 30 seconds, you would set the millisecondsInFuture to 30000.

```
new CountDownTimer(30000, countDownInterval) {
}
```

The second parameter, countDownInterval, specifies when an interval or tickwill be fired. Let's say you want to perform an action, such as updating a screen or checking the progress of an in-game task periodically. You would set the countDownInterval to something less than the millisecondsInFuture, like so:

```
new CountDownTimer(30000, 1000) {
}
```

This code sets up a new CountDownTimer() that will expire in 30 seconds and fire off a tick every 1 second. However, there is a little more coding to do before the timer is complete. You need to override two methods (see Listing 17-1).

Listing 17-1. CountDownTimer()

```
new CountDownTimer(30000,1000) {
@Override
public void onTick(long millisUntilFinished) {

//perform any interval-based calls here
}

@Override
public void onFinish() {

//perform any clean up or ending of tasks here
};
}
```

The first method, onTick(), is called after the expiration of every countDownInterval. The second method that you need to override is onFinish(). The onFinish() method is called after the CountDownTimer() has fully expired.

Finally, use the start() method to start the timer. The start() method is called from CountDownTimer() to activate the timer and begin the countdown (see Listing 17-2).

Listing 17-2. start()

```
newCountDownTimer(30000,1000) {
@Override
public void onTick(long millisUntilFinished) {

}

@Override
public void onFinish() {

};
}.start();
```

One great use for the onTick() method is to write the time to the screen. For example, using the solutions in Chapter 16, you can set up a sprite sheet with the digits 0 through 9. However, rather than keep score, it can be used to count down the time (see Listing 17-3).

Listing 17-3. Displaying time

```
new CountDownTimer(30000,1000) {
@Override
public void onTick(long millisUntilFinished) {

switch(millisUntilFinished){
case(29000):
scoreTile.x = 0; //set the x and y to the location of the
scoreTile.y = 0; //correct sprite sheet image for the time digit
break;

...
}

}

@Override
public void onFinish() {

};
}.start();
```

17.2 Stop the Action When the Time Expires

Problem

The game does not stop when the timer expires.

Solution

Use the onFinish() method of the CountDownTimer() to stop the game when the time expires.

How It Works

To stop the game when the time expires, use the `onFinish()` method to call your closing routine. Looking back at the recipes in Chapter 4, you most likely have an exit routine that is called from the exit button on the game's menu.

You can call this same routine from the `onFinish()` method when the timer expires (see Listing 17-4).

Listing 17-4. Game Exit

```
new CountDownTimer(30000,1000) {
@Override
public void onTick(long millisUntilFinished) {

}

@Override
public void onFinish() {

gameView.exit(); //call the method that you established for exiting the game
};
}.start();
```

17.3 Stop the Timer When a Task Completes

Problem

The game timer continues to run after the player has completed the required task.

Solution

Use the `cancel()` method of the `CountDownTimer()` to stop the timer when the player finishes a task.

How It Works

Your game might be set up in such a way that the player is required to complete a task, or series of tasks, within a given amount of time. The question then is, how do you stop the timer when the tasks are complete?

The `CountDownTimer` contains a `cancel()` method that can be called when you need to stop the timer. The key to using this method effectively is to instantiate a `CountDownTimer` and scope it so it can be called from other methods in your game. Listing 17-5 shows you how to instantiate the `CountDownTimer` (slightly different from how it was done in Recipe 17.1) and then stop the timer using `cancel()`.

Listing 17-5. Cancel CountDownTimer

```
private CountDownTimer cdt;
...
cdt = new CountDownTimer(30000,1000) {
@Override
public void onTick(long millisUntilFinished) {

}

@Override
public void onFinish() {
//something bad happens to the player for failing
};
}.start();

... //rest of your game code

private checkTask(){
//this is a method that you create to check if the player
//has finished the required task
if(taskCompleted){
cdt.cancel();
}
}
```

Index

U

V, W, X, Y, Z

Get the eBook for only $10!

Now you can take the weightless companion with you anywhere, anytime. Your purchase of this book entitles you to 3 electronic versions for only $10.

This Apress title will prove so indispensible that you'll want to carry it with you everywhere, which is why we are offering the eBook in 3 formats for only $10 if you have already purchased the print book.

Convenient and fully searchable, the PDF version enables you to easily find and copy code—or perform examples by quickly toggling between instructions and applications. The MOBI format is ideal for your Kindle, while the ePUB can be utilized on a variety of mobile devices.

Go to www.apress.com/promo/tendollars to purchase your companion eBook.

Apress®
THE EXPERT'S VOICE™